THE FIRE REPLY

Confronting darkness and disease
with *power* and *authority*

THE FIRE REPLY

BENJI RODES

www.churchoftheundignified.com

Cover Design by Matt Larson
Page Layout by Mark Buschgens

ISBN 978-0-9885314-0-6

DEDICATION

This book is dedicated to the Church of the Nazarene, who has poured their prayers, support and love all over me, my family and Church of the Undignified. They have trusted God and trusted us as we have attempted to follow Holy Spirit into the darkness of central Seattle in order to see the realities of heaven erupt upon this amazing city.

ACKNOWLEDGEMENTS

I am so grateful for my wife, Abbi, who has endured on this journey of a lifetime. Your connection and relationship with Holy Spirit has kept me on track and hungering for more of God. You are beautiful, amazing, so talented, and your song writing and voice blow me away, into His presence.

I credit Sam and Snow for helping me know vital aspects of the nature of God, revealing the Father's heart and showing me the kind of faith that is praised in heaven. I thank Church of the Undignified and all the amazing revivalists that are running this race with us. Thanks for your endurance, your faith, your joy and helping turn this Body into a family. The family and true friendship you've built in a culture of honor have made this a movement of significance. Thank you to Landon Snow and Eleven-One Ministries for their partnership in this publication.

Of course, I give a big shout of thanks to Holy Spirit for doing what He does best—leading us into truth, joy and the kingdom of God.

CONTENTS

INTRODUCTION

My wife, Abbi, and I minister in one of most spiritually deprived places on the planet. We're not among the witchdoctors and poverty in Africa. And we haven't put our roots down in the violent Islamic territory of the Middle East. We have established ourselves in central Seattle, starting off in the neighborhood of Capitol Hill. Intellectualism, the occult, materialism, apathy, addiction, brokenness, deceit and religious woundings have combined to create a canyon between this land and divine Love. The man from the Gerasenes in Mark 5, infested with demons, cutting himself with stones and screaming, would have found a good home in Capitol Hill. No one would've bothered him. Such obvious darkness may exist, but when a son or daughter of the King walks on the cement soil of the tortured and broken, the air becomes breathable. The oxygen of darkness is fear, but the presence and power of Jesus' brand of love asphyxiates fear. Where there is no fear we will find a foundational love that is releasing revival. And this happens through *us*. It can happen through you. Even if you are not called to the inner city, the principles of becoming a walking revival are the same. We are powerful. It's part of our trademark as a new creation. Much of my journey in the Christian life seems to consist of learning to release what I've been (re)-born with.

Christians *are* revivals. I am a revival. Anyone who believes is a revival. We carry the life, breath and the power of God. When we cry out for revival we are crying out for God to use us, and people like us. When Jesus had compassion on the multitudes because they were scattered and helpless, He went on to heal everyone. He then explained that the harvest is never lacking and is not the problem. The darkness is not the problem and the darkness certainly is not people. People are the harvest and the darkness is an absence of truth in areas that have not yet been contacted and influenced by a redeemed son or daughter of the King. The lack sleeping beneath our darkest community issues is that there are too few people actually doing the "work"—putting to work the light, glory and authority God has given us—through divine love.

Elijah stepped into a land steeped in the occult and built a stage for the God of Creation to be magnified and proved. "Let me show you!" Paul served the same God, and he came with a demonstration of the Spirit.[1] Jesus, our model for how to live this Christian life, would say, "So that you know I have authority to say what I'm saying, watch this crippled guy get up and walk."

---

[1] 1 Corinthians 2:4

The God who answers by fire is God. God is known as He is shown…*by us*. People again will know that Jesus is who we say He is because we are demonstrating Him in power, signs and miracles.

The disciples were not *allowed* to leave the city with the good news until they had been clothed with power. After Jesus' resurrection they asked Him if He was going to restore the kingdom to Israel now. His reply? "Nope. *You* are going to receive power when the Holy Spirit comes upon you." The subsequent prayer meeting was answered with fire coming down on each person. Contained within the fire that fell on each was the nature and power of God Himself. The invitation to me has been the same: "As you set out to minister, make sure My fire has fallen on your head."

Finding myself in a thick urban cloud of crap, I cried out for God to come and change my city and my neighborhood. His reply was bringing me into a place where I knew I was powerful. I had authority to move in His name. He responded with fire from heaven. But it didn't fall on my city. It fell on *me*! It fell on my family. The fire is consuming the Church of the Undignified and we are going out with a passion for His kingdom and righteousness and the realities of heaven are breaking out on the beloved broken as lives and bodies are healed, people are set free, demons are running and the river of God is going to bury Broadway with life.

I had walked near God for nearly my entire life yet my experience of His power and miracles had been minimal. Becoming convinced that my life was supposed to look like the life of Jesus', I had to find out why so few miracles frequented the ground I walked on. *How* was I intended to powerfully walk in the name of Jesus?

This book details the specifics of our journey out of religious planning and into a ministry of power. Accepting a mission to release light in the devil's playground, we were compelled to discover the power of God and the ministry of Jesus. We became convinced that we were to walk and to heal as Jesus did. We grew in our awareness of the implications of God giving us a new birth from above. We have been recreated into a force on the earth. And where there is light there is no darkness. Where we walk the enemy flees and demons are terrified. We were standing on rebellious soil, but what really needed to be transformed was our faith. This whole book can be boiled down to a revelation of God beckoning us into absurd faith. Without hunger, endurance and an expectant, illogical faith our ministry would remain human and our city hopeless.

As you read, it is my hope that you will be immersed in the fire of His Presence and power, that you come to know that God is objectively good and that you are powerful. God has given you authority and your city is not safe from the kingdom of God being released through you. God is known in your city because you are there manifesting His goodness. In the new nature He's given you, you are capable of performing miracles.

1

LIGHTS ON

The presence of the miraculous stirs up awe, mystery, and it requires that people choose between faith and unbelief.

Coffee Messiah

Welcome to Capitol Hill. This is the historic neighborhood were misfits and rejects have always been accepted, the land where the sacred is profaned and demonical ideas abound. It is an area where the oddest people are not noticed because everyone seems odd and what we think of as normal is deemed bizarre. On any given day, you can see a man on a leash being led by his master, someone shouting at the moon or people in costume except it's not Halloween. It is a bizarre place, where the light of Christ is rarely seen and darkness is prevalent.

During my first few days in the city of Seattle, I wandered by a storefront on Capitol Hill with a sign outside that read "Coffee Messiah". It had a big neon cross above its entrance, the word "sanctuary" scripted on the door frame and a picture of a downcast, thorn-crowned Jesus face on its glass door. I stepped onto a floor painted in flames to see that the whole structure of the interior was crafted to look like a cathedral. Behind the counter hung about forty crucifixes of different styles on a wall of flames. On the large cross in the middle a Pee Wee Herman doll hung crucified. Nearby, another neon sign preached the message, "Caffeine Saves."

I realized that this place was not a Christian coffee shop by any means. After initial offense, I came to understand that I couldn't be upset with a people who didn't have any idea what they were doing. I could guarantee the owner and workers had no real exposure to Jesus Himself embodied in those who went by His name. They'd heard of ideas, religion, hypocrites, and a judgmental walk of shame that others call a way of life. The ultimate question haunted me and would echo in my spirit: How do you reach a people like this?

This coffee shop threw tracks on how to get saved on their café tables as a joke. "How to win a Muslim to Christ" sat on one table. The next table had a track that would appeal to the youth. Another would tap into the atheist mind and lead him to Jesus.

My ideas about potential actions ranged over the natural plane. *Maybe we should start a discussion. Maybe an outreach. Meet needs on the street and in the community. Serve the poor.* I wanted to penetrate the mind of "unbelievers" so as to prod them to think differently about the religion that was still clinging bitterly to the roof of their mouths.

Not knowing where to start, I began with the needs that seemed most obvious and the cultural classrooms that were most revelatory were open mics and sidewalks. My time on the sidewalks was rich simply because God is near to the broken. Wherever we find the broken and dying there will also be an unparalleled measure of His presence.

The Poetry Pulpit

I was a shy kid who believed in the power of God but had never experienced it. And I had been trained for ministry! I had paid good money to be equipped for precisely this day. Classes in missions taught me to learn from the people, so that's what I did. I squatted on the sidewalks with those who lived there and I participated in an open mic poetry reading at Coffee Messiah. I found I could learn more of a person's thoughts on life, God, faith and love through a two-minute piece of prose than I could through years of coffee dates. What one would seldom reveal of their heart one-on-one, they would artistically wax in front of a crowded café.

One by one, the open mic moderator would invite the next person who had signed up to read their work. Of course this messianic coffee shop had a pulpit on hand for people to read behind. So I would stand behind a pulpit and share my thoughts, primarily through surrealism, on my neighborhood and the people I had encountered. My poetry was raw perception of the soil I was called to sow into.

Critical minds, foolish faith, contradictions, stubbornness, fallow ground and the god of this age blinding minds frustrated me to no end. I lived on the "wayside"—the worst place for a seed in Jesus' parable. What hope does a seed have on pavement with so many "birds of the air" (demons) swarming? My ethnographic scribblings became not only a way to relate and connect to the culture but also a great outlet for me as I tried to process my experience in this soil.

The darkness around me was overwhelming. How could someone trained in ministry and missions feel so under-equipped? I wanted to be Jesus and demonstrate His goodness, but honestly, if I was impressed by the darkness then I didn't have a clue about the supremacy and effect of pure Light.

Table Manners

Of those whom I've encountered over the last decade in Seattle, most of the hurting and dying in my city have had experiences with Christianity that have left them hurt, ostracized or abandoned. This has led them to turn both their shoulders cold to the faith founded on love. In my first year on my new mission field I remember so clearly sitting in Coffee Messiah reading a God book before the open mic got started and a guy asked what I was reading. He was one who seemed to epitomize Capitol Hill with his unique, homemade appearance, dark individuality and intellectual pose. His face was pierced and tattooed.

He asked for the title and I told him, "Can Man Live without God?" He smirked with such a demonic arrogance that I shuttered inside. I was so aware of my insufficiency and smallness, feeling completely helpless to "save his soul". Much of my journaling during this season of life and ministry had to do with the darkness around me and I reflected much on this fallow ground and the parable of the sower. I saw myself on the wayside and I seemed to experience every person as being hardened to the core, resistant to God, anti-Jesus and brutal toward followers of the Way.

There is one solution for those whose spiritual woundings have left them, with good reason, calloused to Christ-ians: another experience. Not an argument, explanation or friendship. Jesus never said, "Go, be friends with people." While true friendship is incredibly powerful, the real need is for an encounter with God. Our friendship with the wounded and jaded can be that encounter with God if we are of the brand of believers who know and expect His power to emanate with precision, wisdom and regularity.

First Swing: On the House

Our first organized stab at serving the community came in the form of a free venue we offered to the community. My experience in sitting with the beautiful sidewalk dwellers and warming the Coffee Messiah pulpit with other artists had set me on a mission to demonstrate the good news in a way that would be noticeably different. But one of the many things that I now appreciate about the Capitol Hill neighborhood is that it is nearly impossible for something "different" to get their attention. Some girls from our church dressed up as pirates on a normal weekday, walked the streets for fun and were just people in the crowd. They were unnoticed. During one of our church gatherings at our storefront we saw about 30 naked and painted cyclists coast down our street. Another time, a block over, I saw a guy leading another man on a leather leash in a black leather thong walking over to their favorite bar in daylight. No looks. I began to understand that being different wouldn't accomplish anything.

I knew that the presence of the real kingdom of God would get attention in this neighborhood, but how? One theme I noticed in this "anything goes" neighborhood was that most of the activity was self-serving. It had not yet been revealed to me that the miracle power of God was in me, so providing a selfless service that would meet a practical need in this neighborhood became my ambition. Selfless service was as foreign on Capitol Hill as the sight of my family holding hands walking down Broadway, Capitol Hill's main strip. I remember picking up some Pho' (an Asian noodle soup dish) on Pike Street when my daughter, Snow, was small. A guy saw us and gasped to his friend, "A baby!" How amazing is that? A baby seen on Capitol Hill! Just the presence of a normal family caught their attention and shifted their awareness towards the kingdom of light.

One of the needs of this neighborhood was a place for the arts. Open Mic events were constantly getting kicked out of coffee shops. Apparently, freeloaders and loud noise over an entire evening wasn't good for business. Painters needed a space to display. Filmmakers needed a screen for viewings, dancers a place to dance. Improvisational movement needed an open floor. Loners and the homeless needed a community living room where they could be without having to rent a table with a purchase of a drip coffee. So, we opened Seattle's first-ever free arts venue.

We named this space, "On the House". It meant, "free". This, to us, was synonymous with grace. Whatever event was taking place on whatever night was what the space was for. It was offered for free, there was no cash register in the building, and we used this space to attempt to serve, bless and meet a need in our neighborhood. Abbi, my wife, opened a photography studio in part of the space so we could pay the high rent that was required. We photographed weddings together and she used her many skills to tap the creatively-starved industry for some unique offerings that helped make it possible for us to afford to be there.

This "community living room", as we called it, was situated between an art gallery and a yoga studio. While in the upstairs office space I could hear the classes behind the next wall calling out to other gods. Eerie. On the other side of our space the gallery paraded visual art that was overtly demonic and pornographic. Although we were not an organized church, we were a handful of believers serving the community and that made us a church. The church was birthed out of On the House's service to the community. But what began as a service needed to become a penetrating force.

The Clash

One of the shows of the gallery next door to On the House was called, "The Art of the Tarot Card". With a title like that we felt the need to have a meeting of our own. We could not sit by as the enemy set up a worship gathering of his own right next door to us. We were friends with the owners and operators of this gallery, and we were not fighting against them but against the influence that was pouring forth from their business. We would pray blessing and prosperity over them, but the current content of their enterprise would have to change. We scheduled a night of intercession for the night of their show.

The gallery had provided the community with many services besides visual art. There were frequent burlesque shows and even a "Blood-Letting Conference". During this conference the instructor, every visible part of her skin tattooed with spider webs, educated the people on how to orally draw blood from another person's neck. Training for modern day vampires was occurring next door to people who were convinced that a re-presentation of shining Light would dispel and cancel such darkness.

The gallery set up for their show as DJs rolled their equipment in and others set up the bar. They packed out their space and it was hopping with activity. Ten of us paced our space and began to pray, declaring the Words of God and coming against the darkness. Putting our hands on the walls, we released Light. We eventually just put on a CD and went into some worship. The CD repeated several times as we just lost it in celebratory worship, dancing around, goofing off and having a blast in the presence of God.

Attendees of the "cool" party next door began to wander over to our space, asking what was going on. Three people who had attended the Tarot Card art show became regular, key people of Church of the Undignified. That art show was the last one for that gallery as they went out of business that month. While we mourned with the owners, we celebrated the victory of Light in our neighborhood. It was during this season of our presence in this neighborhood that God began to reveal to us the principles of dominion and how much power for influence He has put upon the those who go by His name and venture to believe all that He has said.

I'm Not Ready for This!

Abbi and I were slowly (I felt) being equipped to minister in power. It was all happening very quick, but I still felt so inadequate. Because of who was coming to our church services and where we were located, in a storefront on Capitol Hill, there was never a boring Sunday morning. Atheists and addicts, full-on Jews and self-proclaimed heathens would attend. A guy came in one Sunday with a Samurai sword strapped to his back. During teachings, people would start convulsing as they went into withdrawals from addiction, or fall asleep due to diseases, and a variety of others would pop in from the nearby Seattle Mental Health. The needs were thick.

One Sunday, a woman was receiving prayer after church. She was sweet, broken, in need and ready for change. A few people started to pray a bit and something in this woman began to react. The prayers were not aggressive but the Holy Spirit is not a passive God. When His presence comes and when "Jesus" is welcomed, hell can break loose. The woman began to shake, spittle developed on the corners of here mouth, her nose started to bleed and she asked, "What's happening?!" as she has lost control of her body. The team praying for her had no idea what to do. Abbi came up in front of the woman, took her by the hands, looked her in the eyes, called her by name and told her to come back. She settled down as the demon stopped throwing a fit.

I had not been equipped for this kind of ministry yet. This woman had been through nearly everything you could think of. Most of what we knew of deliverance came from our Vineyard mentors and Francis MacNutt's book, "Deliverance from Evil Spirits: A Practical Manual". We contacted MacNutt's ministry and they put us in touch with Larry and Audrey Eddings, who currently reside in Silverdale, WA. We brought the woman to their group and I was allowed to sit in on the deliverance. I was in awe as this kind, gentle, elderly man calmly and sweetly led this woman into freedom with his team. With a soft voice and smile, demons would be told to leave, for authority is not recognized by volume.

Months later, while sitting in a car outside our storefront space I made a connection. One of the demons called out by name during the woman's deliverance was also written on the sign of the Yoga studio right next door to our space. They were offering classes under the name of a demon. The business right next to us was giving demons and we were casting them out.

Searching for Ammo

I am married to a "feeler". She can sense things in the Spirit that I simply have no clue about. She can walk into a store and feel oppression and demonic activity that will literally make her nauseas. I'll notice a funny bumper sticker in the same store and not pick up on the presence of angels or demons. Once we step outside, her nausea leaves.

Living in the Capitol Hill neighborhood, notorious for encouraging any and every kind of experimental lifestyle, was oppressive. We both grew up in church and in small towns. In our new, urban environment we felt so under-equipped spiritually. We saw and felt the oppression but felt helpless to bring transformation. Feeling this way is natural and common, but it is not biblical for believers to feel this way when they have been given "authority over all the power of the enemy" (Luke 10:19).

Hungry for ammunition so we could bring His goodness with power, we began to search. We received some great mentoring from Rich and Rose Swetman, Vineyard pastors north of Seattle. We found videos from John Wimber's "Doing the Stuff" series and our church of 12 people would watch a session and then practice listening to God and giving "words of knowledge". We attended a Healing Academy put on by Larry and Audrey Eddings, of the United Methodist Church. We went to a few conferences. We took our church of (now) 20 through inner healing tools to try to get us all free of root problems that keep us from our full potential. The approach was primarily about inviting the Holy Spirit to reveal lies we've believed, asking for the truth and going through forgiveness. I went to a healing school at a church in Redding, CA and I was growing more and more excited about Jesus and how He saw me.

All of these things brought us into different anointings, they activated gifts within us and stirred up hunger and boldness in us. Power, faith and confidence were being transferred into our veins as we were around people and teachers who were experiencing miracles.

Decision Time

It seems that the Western church of Jesus is perpetually reaching crossroads where we need to choose what kind of Body we will be. Will we do good works or God-works? By "good works" I am referring to a human definition on the level of natural goodness, not the biblical standard of "good works" which was thoroughly miraculous. Good works are good deeds done by nice and thoughtful people, while God-works are flowing through people who are moving in the power of the Holy Spirit, demonstrating that the kingdom of God is indeed nearby. Good works will cause applause while God-works bring people to a point of decision as they are confronted with the reality of heaven, God's kingdom. They will cause offense or they will cause people to "praise your Father in heaven" as they see your kind of goodness.

In Acts 8 people were listening to all that Philip was saying because of all the miracles he was doing. At the end of the day it is said that there was great joy in that city because of Philip's presence, words and the power of God moving through his obedience and faith (vv. 6-8). Moving in the power of God quickly eliminates the middle ground of indecision and apathy. Jesus moved in power and people begged him to leave their area. More often, the ones who encountered His goodness went back to their cities and dragged out every invalid, skeptic, dog and sick person to "come see the one who told me everything I ever did." People are intended to experience the kingdom of God through encounters with His power.

The Full Gospel

The gospel is the "good news". When we proclaim the good news to people we are not only talking about Jesus coming into the world to save sinners. It does not just mean that there has been a way made for us to get into heaven. Remember, Jesus preached the gospel before He was crucified and risen. His message revolved around the good news of the kingdom of God. His kingdom describes an environment where His will is perpetually being carried out. One of the main purposes of God putting on flesh was to bring about a repentance (which literally means a changing of the mind and thoughts) that would enable people to see and encounter God's nature and reality.

Most of the people of my neighborhood are turned off by the story of Jesus. But I believe that *we*, His church, are His current story. While people did not respond to a history lesson on the life of Jesus, they did have a very reflective response to the ministry of Jesus, which calls out the royalty in people and makes the good news manifested with some power.

Jesus always demonstrated what He was teaching. He would talk about the things of the kingdom of God, what life is like when God's will is being done, where His love reigns, and then He would heal and set free every single person who came to Him. When the gospel is fully proclaimed it will include a miraculous demonstration.

A gospel without a demonstration of power is an abbreviated and diluted misrepresentation of God's manner of goodness. If all activity in my ministry can be explained and understood then it does not embody the fullness of the good news. The presence of the miraculous around our church stirs up awe and mystery and requires that people choose between faith and unbelief.

Paul was a raw missionary who excellently modeled what he had been persuaded of concerning how ministry is carried out.

> *For I will not presume to speak of anything except what Christ has accomplished through me, resulting in the obedience of the Gentiles by word and deed, in the power of signs and wonders, in the power of the Spirit; so that from Jerusalem and round about as far as Illyricum I have fully preached the gospel of Christ* (Romans 15:18-19).

This truth in the Word lit my heart on fire. It wasn't on me to try to explain someone into the kingdom. Holy Spirit was on me to demonstrate His reality in His power and with signs and wonders. The kingdom of God is not in word but in power (1 Cor. 4:20) and the fullness of the gospel proclamation is only happening when miracles are present. My religious spirit was fighting this, but truth was becoming exposed before me. Jesus and Paul both lived their lives with this approach: when we go, we go with power.

It may have been pride, but initially I felt guarded against the miracle requirement. It is a bit humbling to come to the realization that I had missed for so long what is perhaps the most obvious aspect of (Jesus') ministry. Any challenge will set you a bit on edge, I guess. But this power requirement was a joyous invitation for me to discover what I am capable of as a believer hosting the very presence, person and power of the Living God. He was inviting me to take Him up on everything that had already been purchased for me.

Compassion Led to Power

The throbbing question that was constantly pricking my spirit was, "How do I confront intense problems like mental illness, cancer, depression, skepticism, etc.?" I believe in love and simply being with people as a comforter and listener in their distress. But this was not a manner of heaven's justice that I see modeled in the New Testament. Showing love through listening to others has produced fruit in my ministry and it will always be a crucial part of a pastoral and missional leader. Yet the virtue of being a good listener did not show me to be a Christian. I don't know if Jesus was a good listener, but I do know He moved in power. Loving in power is a defining element of the person and ministry of Jesus.

After years of service that I would say took place on the human level, according to my natural abilities, it is now unbearable to think about compassion staying on the natural level and the people around me remaining unchanged. I became naïve enough to be convinced that my life was to look like the life of Jesus. Yet nowhere in the gospels do I see Jesus simply being with people in their pain. He did something about it. His compassion led to miracles, healing and deliverance. No reasons were given for people's pain. The pain was immediately relieved. Time and again, we see this being synonymous with proclaiming the good news of the kingdom. It behooves me to pursue this same manner of proclamation.

In the outset I saw myself as an urban missionary who was trying not to presume what danced in the divine mind. I didn't move to Seattle to plant a church but to follow the Holy Spirit and be obedient to whatever He may be saying to me for my new neighborhood. In my depths I would dream big. I could imagine few things on a low level. God's love lives on the world level and I too believed I could change the world. I longed to move in power as my Jesus did. So I tried. And I will keep on trying, growing in my understanding of what it means to do the works of Jesus, moving in power, love and authority. And along the way, I find that I am a walking revival that touches everyone I meet. Along the way, I understand more about certain Scriptures and how to move in Word and Spirit as I am taught more by my perceived failures than by my successes.

The Deaf Get Healed

I remember receiving a frantic call from Bill (not his real name), a member of Church of the Undignified. He and his brother were both making strides to overcome the demon of drug addiction. Both attended the church though his brother, Ted (also not his real name), had been missing for over a year. He had stumbled back into old habits, into fellowship with old friends and found himself on "the wide road".

"Ted's been shot," Bill told me. I went to the hospital and got the story and found a very alive man who was wide-eyed and aligned with God, having escaped death. He and friends were on their way to kill another guy. Ted was driving the car on the vengeful mission while the passengers in the back seat were loading guns. A gun accidentally discharged and the 9mm hollow-point bullet tore into Ted's right ear and out the left side of his nose. The nature of the bullet should have taken the better part of his face off, but it didn't.

Full of life, he recounted the story to me, walking around his hospital bed in his gown, dabbing the blood and saliva from his mouth with the towel around his neck. His half-paralyzed face couldn't contain the saliva or his joy.

He came to church the following Sunday, gave testimony to God's goodness and we all marveled at his story and were glad to have him back. Following the service three of us prayed over Ted and for his hearing to be restored. I struggled to actually believe that he was telling the truth, but even with gauze packed into and over his ear he could hear out of this ear that the doctor had said was completely destroyed. The kingdom of heaven had invaded our storefront in power and completely healed Ted's hearing! I assured myself knowing that you can't fake hearing if you are unable. We would whisper something in that ear and he would respond accordingly. I thought I had believed in healing, but my unbelief was exposed when I saw how surprised I was and how some skepticism and doubt still cluttered my new, God-given nature.

The paralysis eventually left and the hearing remained, and although Ted still, years later, struggles with his sobriety, he is putting up a good fight and he is still full of joy and gratitude, knowing the gospel from experience. His body has felt the effects of the kingdom having come and the gentle nature of the good God who is never angry with His children.[2] I was now living with the shocking revelation that power has been put into the hands of believing followers of Jesus to perform miracles.

Could It Be?

My worldview was quaking. Could it be that this was to be normal? Is it possible that healing power has been made available to believing believers? Is releasing breakthrough and healing to all those in need of it supposed to be the normal method of proclaiming the good news?

I knew that my community was in need of this kind of kingdom preaching. They are in need of a demonstration. Words mean nothing to them. Serving them was meaningful but it did not prove powerful in causing a major shift in their thinking or leading them to a place where they were again willing to revisit the God who had disappointed them through the actions of His followers.

Faith is intended to rest and be founded on the power of God (1 Corinthians 2:5). Lives lacking the gospel's "good" root had polluted and soured most in my neighborhood. And I was in a situation where the task was upon me to live my life in such a way

---

2 Seeing the nature of God through Jesus, I don't believe that God ever gets angry with people. I see Jesus grieve over actions but not get angry. *Kindness* leads to change (Rom. 2:4). Anger did not make the list of the fruits of the Spirit (Gal. 5:22-23).

as to make the "good news" good again. I was to discover "normal Christianity" as modeled by Jesus and let this light go forth.

No Christian Underdog

I was suffocating under the needs and dark chaos of my mission field until I discovered who I am in God. I am powerful, I am light and I am not the underdog in this fight. It was Graham Cooke whom God used to bring me into this crucial revelation. "One in Christ is always the majority." Joshua, the man who took a nation against severe opposition to inherit the promise of God, understood this principle. "One of your men puts to flight a thousand, for the Lord your God is He who fights for you, just as He promised you" (Joshua 23:10). Getting rid of the lying, toxic mentality of the underdog was foundational if I was to experience the fruit I'm ordained to taste (John 15:16).

If God is in me and I feel outnumbered then I am believing a lie and not living in my spirit. They both cannot be a reality. Elisha lived a life governed by what was going on in the Spirit, that's why he could say that the majority was on their side when the enemy encircled his city. He prayed that his fearful servant would be able to see what Elisha saw and God opened his eyes to see the mountain around them covered with horses and chariots of fire all around them (2 Kings 6:14-17).

Holy Spirit seemed to be regularly driving home the truth that darkness *cannot* be around light. It is a contradiction in terms. Where there is shinning light, there is no darkness. Light does not fight with darkness even in the natural. If there is a lamp on in my garage, the garage is not dark. I had to change the way I thought about spiritual darkness, and this took place only as I began to understand the nature of Light.

When I lived more aware of the power of the enemy and his influence in my neighborhood I felt crushed. My perception actually kept vital truths from being my experienced reality. The key transformation that was needed had already been divinely decided: While I was praying that the darkness would change, Holy Spirit was interceding for me to know who I am in Christ. Holy Spirit is always interceding for us, praying and declaring God's will over us (Romans 8:26-27) and I caught the sound of their conversation over me. My mindset had to be replaced with the royal identity that is ours as sons and daughters of the King. He is mighty to save and we have reserved seats in His throne room.

Becoming believers in what has been accomplished for us through the resurrection of Jesus and the gift of the Holy Spirit makes "Your kingdom come" inevitable. Once we agree with the glorious nature of the new creation it will no longer be a stretch to believe for cities and nations to be swimming in the realities of heaven. So let's take a glance at some power endowments that come with being "born from above". Let's look at who Jesus says YOU are.

2

YOU ARE GREATER THAN YOU REALIZE

Regenerated humanity is not only capable but responsible for the amount of heaven that is upon the earth. These re-created people now have DNA that contains the strands of God Himself.

Seattle's spiritually oppressive cloud cover pushed us to discover what is hidden inside the new creation and the kingdom of God. Holiness and righteousness became synonymous with power and we started to see ourselves as God does. Rather than being captivated by the overwhelming needs surrounding us, we could walk confidently as those who carry the light of the world and overcome the darkness.

Christ in You Shifts the World

One day, Abbi was walking down Broadway, Capitol Hill's main strip, praying silently to God. From across the street, a troubled man pointed at her and shouted, "Shut up!" Carrying the presence of God in us and on us will be noticeable. Demons cried out when Jesus was near and that reaction is still occurring. A holy life stirs waters. Righteousness enables your light to shine and shift the atmosphere around you.

Fewer things are of more importance to God than having His people established in righteousness. "Righteousness" and "righteous" are used 173 times in the New Testament, more than "salvation" and "love" (agape) combined. Obviously, an understanding of why the subject is dealt with so heavily has to be of interest to us. "**We are created to be like God in true righteousness and holiness**" (Ephesians 4:24), and He will not rest until our righteousness shines (Isaiah 62:1). This "righteousness" is synonymous with glory and it is something that is visible (62:2). God has paid for it and He is determined to get out of His people all that He paid for. He has provided for it and He is restless until we are walking in all that He has sacrificed to give us.

What does "it" look like? The effect of our brightness and rising is described in Isaiah: "Nations will come to your light and kings to the brightness of your rising" (60:3). To the degree that we believe and rise and shine will determine the degree of our effectiveness in our cities. We have to believe higher and rise up with expectancy and power. We were never intended to simply have a subtle effect on our world. Jesus became sin and was punished for us that we may be clothed with the very glory and righteousness of God[3] in such dramatic fashion that entire nations and rulers see the King's goodness on us and come to us like a flood.

This is an exciting hour to live. A dividing line is being drawn and the people of God are being called up to a higher level (the normal standard of Christian life) to make God manifest. Just as Paul said He came "with a demonstration of the Spirit" we also have always been intended and re-created to reveal and demonstrate the reality of God's power and presence. If you heal the sick or cast out demons then people will be faced with a decision, having witnessed the kingdom come. They will either reject what they have seen or they will marvel and praise God who has given such authority to men (Mt. 9:8).

Our "shining" has little to do with Sunday mornings. Our shining has its most drastic effect as we are going about our day and running into people who are in crisis. Our glory meets their need and people will know God is God. Yes, it is our glory. Isaiah 62 makes it clear that it is *our* salvation, *our* righteousness and *our* glory. It does not say that people will see *His* glory. It is not humility to say that you are not glorious if God says that you are and it is your glory that will cause nations to be saved. Unbelief renders the promises ineffective (Hebrews 4:2). Undoubtedly, it is because of God that we have a visible glory on us. It is God who has glorified us, making us glorious (Isaiah 55:5), which in turn has made us more than fruitful and effective on the earth.

---

[3] 2 Corinthians 3:9-11; 5:21; John 17:22

Many times when we step out to directly shine light onto a need we don't see anything shift or change right then and there. But there are times when you step into a need and you can see the astonishment of people as they just experienced a miracle.

One time, while checking out at a grocery store, the lady in front of me was complaining to the checker about how her knee was in a lot of pain and that she was going to have to have surgery soon. With her permission I briefly released healing and told the pain to leave. She looked up in shock noticing that the pain had left. Our world still does marvel when they experience that God still gives authority to humanity.

"If I cast out demons by the Spirit of God then the kingdom of heaven has come upon you" (Mt. 12:28). Power is what marks Christian goodness and separates it from philanthropy. The former pulls the kingdom of heaven onto the ground we walk on while the latter may possibly be indecipherable from any common humanitarian outreach.

You are Holy and Powerful

One of the first times I really stepped out to offer healing to someone, I was walking over to On the House. God brought to mind a barista at a café I went to frequently. She had shattered her heel and was under the prognosis that it would take months to fully heal. I eventually developed enough courage to go see if she was working. She was. But now *I* needed the busy line to dwindle down. It did. I walked up to the counter and asked her if she would like healing prayer for her heel. She was blessed by the offer. It pains me to say this now, but I didn't pray for her right then. I invited her to a gathering we were having that night. Her countenance changed when I extended the invitation. She never came.

For so long I operated without the understanding that God was on me to bring healing, His kingdom, justice, peace and joy to those around me.

His righteousness is everything that is good and right. It is the environment of heaven. It is the thrill of His perfect will. And it only brings joy, goodness, peace and life. This is the air of His kingdom. The righteous will bring the atmosphere of heaven to earth and will exercise dominion in our cities. But we are given authority in order to serve. We are to serve in power and this is called "ruling". "Those who receive the gift of righteousness will reign in life" (Romans 5:17). If we will receive, by agreement, the gift of righteousness that was extended to us by the shed blood of Jesus, then we will be the righteousness of God (thinking, feeling, and acting as God does) and exercise His dominion, rulership and kingship on earth. We will heal diseases, deliver people from demons of oppression and addiction and establish an air of love in our nations. If this seems too lofty we need to repent—change the way we think. The beating and murder of Jesus was for more than just our salvation. It was also to remake us and restore us into His image that we may restore the ruined cities.

Of course it is not likely to be our experience that once we believe something we see it immediately become an undeniable or consistent reality. Belief in something launches us into a process whereby we are to water through faith the seed of the kingdom principle that we have just received. Constant use, faith and exercising the gift or revelation causes it to grow and mature and become something that will eventually be made known with consistency. We may all have the gift of healing, but not regularly praying for the sick will leave this gift idle and immature in our lives. By the implications of faith, if we believe that we do have the gift of healing and we know that our prayers are powerful, we will naturally be excited and desire to pray for the sick.

You are "Anointed"

It is redundant to say that a Christian is anointed. The word "Christian" we have used to name those who follow and are modeled after the Christ, which means "anointed one". To be Christian is to be anointed by God. "To anoint" (creo) is defined as

a) consecrating Jesus to the Messianic office, and furnishing him with the necessary powers for its administration
b) enduing Christians with the gifts of the Holy Spirit[4]

To be Christian is to be filled with the power of God and endued with the gifts of the Holy Spirit. 2 Corinthians 1:21 states that it is God who has anointed us. He has given us His Holy Spirit and an anointing which has furnished us with the powers and gifts necessary to carry on doing what Jesus was doing on the earth in

[4] http://www.blueletterbible.org/lang/lexicon/lexicon.cfm?Strongs=G5548&t=NASB

His Isaiah 61:1 anointing—setting captives free, bringing healing, deliverance, truth and liberty. It is humbling to think that we have been made capable of carrying on the ministry of Jesus in the same way that He ministered. But it's very true. And it is not humility to say that we are not powerful or not anointed when He says that we are. The best we can do is agree with Him saying, "May it be as you have said."

We are completely dependent upon God and have no life apart from Him. But we must move on from the basic truths of the Christian faith—Christ is in us and God's own Spirit has been put within us. For the sake of our cities we cannot afford to stay in a mindset that confesses our powerlessness. It is entirely true that we have no life or power apart from God. But once I received Jesus it would be doubt and unbelief to continue thinking that I am powerless or can have no effect on my world. If it was God's responsibility to save the world why did Jesus send us out to disciple and teach the nations?

In his letter to the Corinthians Paul explains this dynamic of being people who demonstrate the power of the new covenant. "Not that we are adequate in ourselves to consider anything as coming from ourselves, but our adequacy is from God, who also made us adequate as servants of a new covenant" (2 Corinthians 3:5-6). Firstly, this clearly points out that our adequacy and sheer ability is not coming from ourselves. But listen to the truth this is followed by: our adequacy is from God, who has made us adequate. This is saying that we have been made sufficient and capable to carry out God's commands and will. We have been anointed, and thereby blessed, made capable and powerful to bring the reign of God to the earth.

This is the power and definition behind the Christian life. Any other attribute, virtue or description of the Christian life follows this "anointing". The point and defining key of the Christian life is not purity or sacrifice. What sets "anointed ones" apart is the fact that the Spirit of God has been given to them without measure (John 3:34) and they have been equipped to supernaturally bring the elements of the kingdom of heaven into our world. This is being salt and light. This is being holy as He is holy—demonstrating His nature in the same manner that Jesus demonstrated what the Father is like.

You are Righteous

We carry the same Spirit, glory and righteousness that Jesus did. The attributes and virtues that comprise the nature of God and define Him have been given to us. In His image we were made.

Following Jesus means that we will be like Him, for "everyone, after he has been fully trained, will be like his teacher" (Luke 6:40). God is righteousness and Jesus was righteousness personified. This means that He only thought and did what was right. Jesus was referred to as "the Righteous One" (Acts 3:14) and as Christians we are to be righteous ones also. The theme of "the righteous" as it is followed throughout the life of Jesus and His followers will leave you convinced of God's heart for us. Righteousness is the image and nature of God. Adam had it then lost it. Jesus came with it and restored it to us. The kingdom of heaven is a matter of righteousness and Jesus came to fulfill all righteousness (Romans

14:17; Matthew 3:15).

God burns for us to be restored to the image of pure righteousness, so much so that He would send Jesus to become sin "that we may become the righteousness of God" (2 Corinthians 5:17). Did you hear that? The reason that Jesus took the weight of the world's sin and was buried in His death was so that a way would be made for us to become God's righteousness. His death and resurrection initiated a process whereby a new kind of people are to arise on the earth with His nature, carrying His power and authority and the ability to bring His kingdom to earth.

We are the righteousness of God! Unless, of course, we don't believe we are. That's how relational this faith is. Without faith, the promises and truths of God will lack active power and reality in our lives (Hebrews 4:2).

The earth groans for God's true sons and daughters to arise in faith, agreeing with all the absurd things that He says about us—we are His righteousness and we have His same Spirit, glory, joy, peace, power and authority. That's what the Book says. It simply cannot be stated enough: unbelief gouges us of power and the transforming influence we are intended to have upon our neighborhoods, cities and the ends of the earth.

You Can Release the Power of God Unto Salvation

It does not happen as often as I would like, but every now and then we have people come to Church of the Undignified for the first time and have Holy Spirit come on them in power and bring physical healing to their bodies. One young gal went through a prayer line when church was concluding. One of the pray-ers asked her if she had stomach problems. A bit taken back, she concurred. Healing was released into her stomach and she has been fine ever since.

I love those encounters because that is one of the closest pictures of Jesus' ministry. Their physical need is met, *and then* they follow Him (Mt. 20:34).

We love the thought of people, cities and nations flooding into the church and being saved. This passion for His kingdom come is wired into our DNA. But our light "shining" is synonymous with His power flowing out of us in signs, wonders and miracles. Multitudes crowded around Jesus and pressed into His presence to touch Him because "power was going out from Him and healing them all" (Luke 6:19). I don't believe that it is reasonable to expect people to press into church and be attracted to His followers if power is not going out from us. It is the nature of light to emit light, and it is the nature of the new creation to emit power that transforms the problems of neighbors and cities.

Ok, It's True – You are Amazing

Living with faith in the truth that we are a new creation who is like God in righteousness and holiness will lead us to acknowledge that we are amazing. It is our destiny to cause people to marvel at the goodness of God when we are around because we are manifesting

Him. We are to shine, and when we do, people understand what God is like.

Receiving this truth, agreeing with it, allows the truth to have a transforming effect on our lives. Belief enables transformation. Transformation is initiated in our lives when we know how amazing God thinks we are and we agree with Him. We must know the way He sees us and agree with Him, regardless of the way we may feel about ourselves.

In our church community we don't let people get away with talking bad about themselves. Life and death are in the power of the tongue (Proverbs 18:21). God spoke the world into existence and we were made in His image. All this means that our words carry creative (or destructive) power. Being convinced that the sacrifice of Jesus was enough, we are to come into agreement with what He has said. If people come to me and say they feel bad about themselves, it's usually because they're tuned into the wrong voice.

It really devastates me now when people do not know that they are significant. I would say that about 90% of our ministry consists of reminding people of how amazing and powerful they are. There was a homeless man named David who used to come by our apartment several times a week. He was a rare exception in the homeless community because he was a pure loner. I'd give him food every now and then but he usually just wanted to talk or be with someone. He came by one night and buzzed my door at a very inconvenient time. I went outside to find this man just standing there wanting nothing in particular. He was always filthy. The only clean parts were his vivid, green eyes. He stood in front of me with chunks of vomit in his beard. We walked out to the sidewalk and the whole evening turned very divine. It was sunset and there was a light breeze coming down Belmont Ave. I looked into his eyes and asked him if he knew what his name meant. He said, "No". I told him it means "Beloved". "Do you know that it's true? That you're loved by God and me?" He smiled, showing the few teeth he had, in amazement and disbelief.

Years later, I was living in another part of the neighborhood, but someone else from our Body had become acquainted with David and brought him to church. It was only two weeks after his visit that he died. I don't quite know what to make of it still, but as soon as he was connected to a community, he went straight to be with Jesus. I was so thankful for how our Body responded to this man whose glory had been covered in dirt and many forms of brokenness. He was loved and his was the only memorial service we have ever held in Church of the Undignified.

Righteousness is the nature of God and it gives life and meaning to all it touches. This is why the subject of righteousness is so focused on in the New Testament. Believers have been re-created after God in righteousness; we have been made the righteousness of God; the righteous reign in life; and the kingdom of heaven is a matter of righteousness (Romans 14:17). Jesus gives this subject so much emphasis and priority because so much is hinged upon us becoming the righteousness of God. Confessing, "only God is holy" is a half-truth that dismisses the effect Jesus' resurrection had on those who would believe in Him. If only God is holy then His goodness will never been seen on the earth. We are His very own Body. Living from the truth of our significance will lead to a significant effect on the earth. If we are not holy then there is no light and no hope on the earth.

You can be both Hungry and Satisfied

Jesus explains in one brief sentence that in this life no one will be satisfied or fulfilled except for those who are hungering, thirsting and pursuing righteousness (Matthew 5:6). Our deepest desires will only be satisfied as we go after what we were made to enjoy—the fullness of God's nature and presence living within us. This is righteousness—correct thinking, feeling and acting. Did that sink in? It is only the people who are desperately going after the fullness of His nature being made visible in their lives who will be satisfied.

Feeding the poor is great and we should all do it, but it will not give us satisfaction. Being active in church and giving our lives for others is His will, but it will not fulfill us. We are satisfied and fulfilled as we hunger and thirst for righteousness. The journey that pursues His holiness fills us with heavenly significance. Jesus also emphasized the priority of righteousness when He told us that all of our concerns and desires would be met as we are primarily focused on His kingdom and His righteousness (Mt. 6:33). Our first pursuit has to be His kingdom (His reign, rule and the realities of heaven being made the new normal on earth) and His righteousness in our lives. We are supposed to think, feel and act as God does and all provision has been made for this to be a reality thanks to the resurrection of Jesus and the indwelling presence of the Holy Spirit.

My son, Sam, was born at 6:33 in the morning. Whenever I see a digital clock read 6:33 I am fueled with a fire and immediately brought into a deeper state of prayer and declaration. I live to see His kingdom come and His righteousness on me. Since this has become my primary pursuit I have lived so thrilled in my walk with God. I live anticipating huge moves from heaven, expecting miracles and knowing that God is likely to use me powerfully each and every day. "Seek first His kingdom and His righteousness" (Mt. 6:33). Pursue this. Make this a priority. Go after it with all that you are and you will be satisfied. The journey of faith into this call of righteousness and true holiness is so rich that the mere pursuit will fill you with satisfaction because you will be in the center of His will.

Heaven's Resources are at your Disposal

Believing that we are light and have His same glory (Matthew 5:16; John 17:22) really made me nervous at first. I felt like I was taking credit that only belonged to God. Yet when it is played out as it is intended, our shining ends with everyone singing "To God be the glory". Believing that I am powerful leads me to attempt to release the life and the power of God. When I venture to do so, it usually ends with both parties giving praise to God.

There have been certain seasons for Abbi and me where we will just give cash away to strangers. I once carried $100 in my bag for a week or so, forgetting about it or not being prompted to give it away. Then, when I was checking out at Safeway, I remembered the money in my bag. I knew immediately it was for the cashier. I was nervous because I didn't want the young girl to think I was hitting on her or anything. I asked her a few questions and then told her that I felt like God wanted me to give her this, and I handed her an envelope. She was surprised, confused and thankful, not even knowing what was in it. When I went through her line months later she excitedly told me that the day I gave the money to her she had just lost her purse and her phone. She was broke and had just been calling out to God for help when I came up and handed her an envelope full of cash. We *both* thanked God!

We need God desperately every moment of the day. Without Him we can do nothing. The poor in spirit, those who live with the deep awareness of their need, have ownership of the realities and dominion of heaven (Mt. 5:3). I'm not saying that we don't need God, because *we* are now the light of the world. I am saying that because we live needing God, heaven's resources are at our disposal (power, authority, influence).

You are a Revival

It's unnatural for a Christian not to desire revival, which is God's kingdom come to earth. We're to pray for His kingdom to come and we're to look to bring it in every circumstance and opportunity of our lives. My error has tended to consist of a mindset that put all the responsibility on God, thinking that if nothing is happening then God needs to do more. But due to the power, authority and responsibility that is handed to Christians, scripturally, if nothing is happening to the present darkness, then it is far more likely to be a commentary on our light, not on God's inactivity or "sovereign will". He's put His Holy Spirit in us, which means that we can now release His presence and goodness on the earth. We've been made in His image and made ministers of this new covenant and reality of the kingdom of heaven.

We need a renewed mindset, which acknowledges that regenerated humanity is not only capable but responsible for the amount of heaven that is upon the earth. These re-created people now have DNA, which contain the strands of God Himself.

When our light shines people feel love and the concern of God Himself. There was a woman who wept at the end of one of our Sunday gatherings. Abbi went over to pray for her and felt like God was saying, "He's sorry about your loss." Abbi relayed the message and learned that the woman was weeping because her girlfriend had just broken up with her. It was so awesome that God cared about her brokenness and pain, even if it was stemming from a misguided relationship. God is not out to change us. He has set out to reveal His love and we are changed under the umbrella of love.

Following the disciple's instructions to "beseech the Lord of the harvest to send out workers into His harvest" (Matthew 9:38) Jesus then commissions the disciples and equips them as workers. And what are the workers supposed to do? "Heal the sick, raise the dead, cleanse the lepers, cast out demons" (Mt. 10:8). This is the work of the kingdom and the means to revival. And this job description is something we do. We're not to pray that God does these things. From Jesus' own mouth He says that we're supposed to do these things. We are intended to respond to the call, move in power and usher in *His* harvest.

During a 4-year period when we lived right by Safeway it was a kingdom playground. Crazy awesome things would take place when I went there to just do regularly shopping activity. On one occasion, my son and I came across a woman asking for money. She was stranded in Seattle, trying to get home. She was an emotional wreck, pregnant, rejected and in pain from being on her feet all day on a bad ankle. My son was just a one-year-old. I held him in one arm and pulled Marlene in with the other arm to tell her how amazing God thought she was. Sam and I prayed for her ankle and the pain left. We walked with her toward my house and gave her $20 so she could get home. That encounter with Marlene marked me. She was touched emotionally and physically. She got what she needed in the natural *and* in her physical and emotional pain.

Your Prayers are Powerful

Learning the power of righteousness had a great impact on how I saw the effectiveness of my prayers. The benefits of righteousness exceeded whatever I could imagine. It is promised to change cities, nations and rulers. And the prayers of the righteous are said to be incredibly powerful and they bring immeasurable victory and change. The second part of James 5:16 explains, "The effective prayer of a righteous man can accomplish much." It is a complex, abnormal sentence and thought as it has only five words and two of them are two different verbs describing power and force that is actively working. Another word is translated "a lot", one is "righteous person", and one is "prayer".

It's as though James comes to the subject of righteousness and prayer and cannot come up with a sentence that flows well enough to describe how tremendous it is and the effect that it has. He seems to stammer and bluntly state that the prayers of righteous people wield power, exert force and bring a lot of change. One of the verbs used (ἰσχύει) is defined as:

> "to be strong; to have power; to have power as shown by extraordinary deeds; to exert, wield power, to have strength to overcome; to be a force, avail."[5]

All that is encompassed in one verb.

The previous verb is used alongside another verb, which is translated "works powerfully". And both these actions are followed by "a lot" (or "much"). When righteous people approach God with requests, heaven shifts, His kingdom comes, heaven responds.

James follows his brief explanation of the effect of our prayers by giving us an example. "Elijah was a man with a nature like ours, and he prayed earnestly that it would not rain and it did not rain on the earth for three years and six months. Then he prayed again and the sky poured rain and the earth produced fruit" (James 5:17-18). If righteous people can affect the weather pattern for years, and this is the precedent for our prayers, then we should not only be drawn to pray continually and often but be convinced that our righteousness has an explosive effect on the earth. Righteous

---

[5] http://www.blueletterbible.org/lang/lexicon/lexicon.cfm?Strongs=G2480&t=NASB

people pray continuously and powerfully, affecting situations. I'll give a blotchy attempt at translating the thought behind this part of James 5:16: My prayers force, avail, power, continuously work effectively in any situation.

Effective prayers flow from people who know who they are—the righteousness of God, holy, loved, royal and entrusted with the keys to the kingdom. It is impossible for a believer's prayer to be ineffective. Unbelief (doubt in who we are as new creations) neutralizes our prayers and strips them of their potential transformative effect. Believing prayer moves heaven and shakes the earth, moves mountains, heals diseases, makes the demons flee and silences the seas.

When we pray for revival what we are really praying is that His kingdom will come to a greater extent. That the realities of heaven will be made manifest, which will eliminate fear, depression, cancer, poverty, violence and any other evil. When His kingdom comes God's presence will be recognized and people will live in awe, joy, peace and love as a result. But the means for this great endeavor is the church rising and shining, bringing healing, deliverance and freedom (good news) to everyone we encounter. When we are praying for revival we are praying for more workers. The direct implication of that prayer is "God, we need more believers." But if all believers do is go to meetings and ask God to do stuff, I'm not sure we'll be any closer to revival. All revivals involve prayer. The startling factor about the current revival around the world is that it is occurring through people who are in cities and villages living out Matthew 10:8--shining, loving, demonstrating the kingdom of God and putting the good and powerful nature of God on display.

We're not waiting for God to do something. This mentality may be one of the most common ways to avoid or miss a move of God. God moves through people. We're to pray for workers (more people like us) and then be the workers who work in power, authority, knowing their identity as sons and daughters of God who have been equipped and commissioned, given not just permission but authority to establish His will on the earth. We don't wait passively. When we wait for the "more" of God and His reality on earth, we do so with violence (Mt. 11:12). There is to be an aggressive nature to our pursuit of God, His reality and that reality being manifested in our cities.

Because I am a revival(ist) who carries heaven within me (Luke 17:21), and that kingdom is intended and given in order that it may shine (to let out), it is natural to deduce that this "shining" will transform and shape the world around us. Transformation around us occurs as we fully agree with the new nature God has put in us and as we creatively and powerfully release the glory of that nature. The journey of discovering how to do this is called the Christian life and it is what Jesus died to deliver to us. This new life cannot be lived effectively apart from the gifts that come from the Spirit. The gifts of the Spirit are the essential equipments released so that (once the gifts are developed, grown and refined) a believer may become a force on the earth.

God is developing a new kind of Christian in these days and they are changing the world. One of the key characteristics of these revivalists is that they know they are revivalists—people with a new, holy and powerful nature that is re-made after the characteristics of God Himself. They also realize that they have been gifted with the privilege of hosting the presence and power of God and they have the opportunity and responsibility to bring heaven to earth. They pray persistently and with passion and they live with a bold faith that costs dearly, demands all and is alive with expectation and reward. That new kind of Christian is you.

3

POWER TO SET THE CAPTIVES FREE

God makes all power available to us, but faith is what makes it accessible.

Sparks Fly

During our years at On the House there was a woman who regularly stopped in. We'll call her Val. We enjoyed her company and we had many open conversations with her. She was a massage therapist who was very spiritual and was undergoing classes in the occult. It was her understanding that when people come to her for a massage then they are giving her permission to also work on their spirit. Her intention was always to help, and as she would see demons on people she would tell them to leave. She admitted that not all of them would leave though.

As Abbi listened to her and began to explain to her the power of Christianity and that when we tell demons to leave, they have to. The woman began to talk about her power and Abbi felt her own guard come up. Abbi noticed that her hands (Abbi's) were in fists on top of one another by her right hip, as if she was holding a sword. As the woman continued to talk Abbi moved into silent prayer and in her imagination she instinctively moved the "sword" up quickly to block what was coming out of our friend. Val exclaimed, "Did you see that?! There was a huge spark in the air." In the realm of the spirit, Abbi's sword was blocking the demonic influence and both parties were aware of it. What Abbi "saw" in the Spirit, as she was moving in her imagination and visualizing the prayers she needed to pray, became manifest. Though we don't wage war as the world does, and our battle is not against people, we do have weapons. We have access to weapons that are powerful against anything that is setting itself up against the knowledge of God and our battle is in the spiritual realm (2 Cor. 10:3-5; Eph. 6:12).

Response Ability

From both camps, that of the enemy and from that of God-lovers, questions and concerns rise over the problem of evil, the issues of death, crime, disease and sickness and we cry out to God for change, intervention and relief. Yet considering what God already has done for us and said to us, I'm beginning to think that such questions and pleas heavenward are now irrelevant. It's not His move. It's ours. It is to us whom the Spirit has been given without reservation. It is we who have been filled with His fullness. It is to us whom all authority has been given. God seems to be looking at us as He did Moses on the other side of the Red Sea as an army pursued them, asking, "Why are you crying out to me? Tell the Israelites to move on" (Ex. 14:15). Divide the waters and go ahead. Go, do the impossible!

His Spirit and anointing are given to us to proclaim and show the good news of great joy. Move on! The kingdom is in you and my Spirit is upon you to set captives free and release those who are bound. It is to us that God says, "Give the mourners beauty, joy and praise to replace their ashes of worthlessness, mourning, and failing spirit." Is this not reminiscent of Jesus' ridiculous request for His disciples to feed the multitude though they had no food? "You give them something to eat." You give people beauty, joy, praise, or whatever transformative element they need. You are able to put that on them and change them into different people. Give it to them "that they may be called trees of righteousness, the planting of the Lord, that He might be glorified" (Isaiah 61:3). To be sure, the Source is and always will be God. But this living God has put His very Spirit and anointing on us, the anointed ones (Christ-ians), in order to accomplish His will for humanity. His Spirit is upon us to do the things that only God can do.

No Conduit, No Power

The power is from God and not from us. Yet we are the conduits for this power. It flows through us, believers, or it doesn't flow at all. At the very least, it is severely limited. Acts 3 illustrates the tension of the source of kingdom power. Peter and John were on their way to a prayer meeting. Imagine this. A lame man is being carried along, notices them, and asks for money. Peter wants the man's eyes. "Look at us!" Eye contact makes it personal, it gave dignity to the man rejected by the world and his miracle was at hand. Notice that Peter and John did not ask God to heal this man. Peter said, "What I have I give to you." The man gets healed! They knew they had something to give. It was in them. Grace, healing and the power of God were given to them to steward and they did just that, knowing the heart and ways of God.

Peter and John did not pray in that moment because they knew what God's will was and that His power was in them. There was no confusion about the Source. They always knew that it was *all* God, yet they also knew that they had unlimited access to this power source. Do you feel some tension? "Why do you marvel at this? Or why do you look so earnestly on us, as though by our own power or holiness we had made this man to walk" (Acts 3:12)? It was all God, yet they knew He was in them, they had authority, and they had it to give.

Receiving the truth that I was powerful landed me in a tension. It was much easier to live thinking that I just had to pray and it was God's responsibility to do everything else. Believing I was given power and authority complicated things a bit and I was driven into His presence to find out more. Under the guidance of the Holy Spirit I needed to feel my way through this paradox and become a true *believe*-r. At deeper and deeper levels I needed to accept that I am who God says I am. I am a new creation, born from above, a representative from another kingdom who has been equipped with everything I need to establish heaven on earth. Remember, we have been made capable to be ministers of the new covenant (2 Cor. 3:6).

When I go to God with a problem I often feel Him look at me with a smile and respond, "Why are you asking me about this? I'm on you and in you. You're more than equipped. Go heal cancer, move mountains, multiply food, walk on water, raise the dead. Do you not know that my Spirit is upon you and you've been anointed for such things?"

The promise hangs unavoidable. The following verse is too absurd yet also too clear. There's no other interpretation. "Nothing is impossible for those who believe" (Mark 9:23). Do we believe we are as powerful as He says we are? Undoubtedly, the difficulty in accepting the new paradigm Jesus introduced is why the primary message coming with the New Covenant was, "Repent", which means, "think again". Change the way you think because things are not the way you thought— "God's not mad, heaven is near, I've given you a new nature and you are powerful to break impossibilities!"

Bridging the Gap

For six years Abbi and I served people by giving them a venue for nearly any form of art. We gave drinks to the thirsty, listened to the lonely and saw many turn toward God. The model of love and service we operated out of did cause my community to grow with awe and skepticism concerning such kindness. They didn't know how to translate grace. They had no grid for goodness. They applauded such sacrifice as we gave of our bodies, our time and resources in order to bless our neighborhood and meet needs that they had. Abbi and I started a photography business and we photographed weddings together so we could pay the high rent for the storefront venue we were giving to the community.

This kind of love and service is no doubt good. I believe God smiled upon it. He blessed our business and supported our dreams as we ventured out, risked and did the best we knew to do in order to try to somehow make manifest the goodness of God. Yet the problem with our kind of service, I became convicted, was that it lacked power. While we did need God in order to make it happen, that was not what was apparent to the community. The people we served thought we were nice folks. The fact is that anyone from any belief system on the planet with a few resources could have done most of what we were doing. They could do it without the presence and power of God. This was unnerving.

Striking a Nerve

In Seattle it didn't take me long to come to the understanding that it would take more than an invitation to get someone to see the appeal of the kingdom. The message of the kingdom produced a massive shift in my thinking, my spirit and my approach to ministry. In proclaiming the message of the kingdom, God was inviting me to demonstrate His goodness with power. One of the first prophetic words spoken over my life to my parents was that I would be a great evangelist. The idea of being an evangelist did not cause much excitement in me. To me, at the time, it just meant that I would probably just be preaching to people or doing some sort of street ministry trying to get people to say a prayer.

This sort of approach to ministry revolves around the gospel of *salvation*, as we are just trying to get people "saved". Jesus came proclaiming and demonstrating the gospel of the *kingdom*. Salvation is included in the gospel of the kingdom but the gospel of the kingdom spreads far wider than just getting someone into heaven. We have a show-and-tell gospel that is intended to carry a power encounter with it.

"My message and my preaching were not in persuasive words of wisdom, but in demonstration of the Spirit and of power" (1 Cor. 2:4). For me it was a huge relief to know that I did not have to try to convince the people out here to give Christianity another shot. Most of the people I was around had experienced Christianity already. It did not go well. My spirit leapt as I received Paul's words and got a revelation of how he went about doing ministry. It had nothing to do with persuading people and giving a sermon of wisdom. His message was contained in a demonstration, a proof, of the Spirit. He would actually make the Spirit, God Himself, visible and obvious through a move of power. This was his approach to ministry.

Believe Because of the Works

I was invited by a friend to share about miracles with a group he regularly met with. It was a very intellectual group that consisted of mostly unbelievers, many atheists and many of them used to go to church when they were young. My friend began the discussion, which addressed matters that related to spirituality, in order to help build relationships and bridges into life. I gave a brief, 30-minute teaching on the kingdom of God, how Jesus and the disciples did ministry, the power of God and the ministry of healing. After some Q and A we went on to step out and demonstrate the good news, believing that if there is no power present then we're not talking about the kingdom (1 Cor. 4:20).

We prayed for a guy's back but he was not able to test it there to see if it was actually better. Then a man who had been mostly quiet piped up. Holding up a hand with a missing finger, he professed, "If you cause my finger to grow out, I'll be a better believer than you." I, along with a few of my friends who came, gathered around the man and told the finger to grow out in Jesus' name, as a room scattered with agnostics and atheists watched. The stage was set and we did what we felt Jesus would be doing. Nothing happened. The finger did not come back. But I was still fully convinced that this was the manner of ministry that our "good news" is founded on. It flows from a demonstration. I told that group that they did not have to believe anything I was saying if they did not see a miracle. Without power the message is just another philosophy or argument to them.

The faith of the followers of Jesus is supposed to rest on the power of God and not the wisdom of man (1 Cor. 2:5). Jesus Himself said, "If I do not do the works of My Father, do not believe Me; but if I do them, though you do not believe Me, believe the works, so that you may know and understand that the Father is in Me, and I in the Father" (John 10:37-38). Jesus invited the people around Him to verify His ministry by His miracles and I am living toward that same standard.

Power is Miraculous

God's kingdom is in power. This word "power" is the same word that is translated "the effecting of miracles" in the gifts of the Spirit (1 Corinthians 12:10). If I am talking about the kingdom of God, the gospel, to my community then there will be a demonstration of power. It is possible to do nice things with a very pure heart, as I believe we had done early on in our ministry. But scripturally I cannot refer to what I did as "kingdom" since there was no power. The gospel of the kingdom that Jesus spoke was not "I am going to die on a cross for your sins." Don't get offended here. I am helpless without the death and resurrection of Jesus and His payment for my sin. I've given my life to Him because of this great historical truth. But this was not the gospel message He was giving. Remember, Jesus was preaching the gospel prior to His death, so the gospel of the kingdom must mean more than "Jesus died on the cross for our sins, to restore us to right relationship with God." Jesus revealed the true nature of God and He came explaining God's realm—His kingdom, His domain. When His will is always being done this is what it looks like... As He preached this He healed everyone who came to Him, demonstrating what His kingdom looks like...in power.

I'm beginning to question whether or not someone can hear

the gospel, the good news of the kingdom, and not experience it simultaneously. If "the kingdom of God is not in word but in power", what else could this suggest? I needed to change the way I was thinking about the "gospel" and not reinterpret 1 Corinthians 4:20 and Matthew 10:8 in order to justify my feelings of powerlessness. The good news says that the Spirit in me will bring about miracles, signs and wonders; healings and deliverances will occur with great frequency and the faith that this produces in those who experience it will cause them to place their new faith on the power of God rather than man's wisdom.

Walking in the kind of power Jesus does proves difficult, obviously, but I realized that the main obstacle of this lifestyle was my own logical thinking (a.k.a. unbelief).

Is Logic Illogical?

The moment we receive Jesus and the Person of the Holy Spirit we are ushered into a new realm—the spiritual life. In this new, more real, world we are required to think in a new light and see things as God Himself sees them. In the pursuit of "the more" that is promised to the believer as an inheritance and as part of this new creation, many roadblocks surface. The main roadblock will be our own thinking, and most will side with our appetite for the familiar. Jesus compared our desire for new things with how people generally respond to wine. "No one, after drinking old wine wishes for new; for he says, 'The old is good enough'" (Luke 5:39). It may be true that, "The taste for truth is an acquired taste, that few acquire."[6]

Living with God's gift of the mind and simultaneously pursuing a spiritual life is more than challenging. God will often speak something to us that, without spiritual eyes, we will miss, call illogical or flat-out false. A lie. We are required to hear and believe on a different plane. To attempt to live the spiritual life in the natural will create a schizophrenic believer who is double-minded, attempting to live the spiritual life on natural principles, with natural senses. *This* is illogical. We are required to live by the unseen.

If we follow God's ways with the mind of Christ, then we, too, will call the things that are not as though they were (Romans 4:17). God walks around seeing things as He wills them, or as they are becoming, and He will refer to these things as they *will be* and not as they currently are. Any "sane" person would say that this practice is crazy—you're a fanatic living in fantasy and not in reality. Such is the invitation to those who will shape the course of history. All world-changers will be led into an illogical dilemma, where once faith and perseverance have finished their work, they will, like Abraham, inherit what is promised. Abraham believed against hope, when everything in the natural contradicted the word over his life, "so that he might become a father of many nations according to that which had been spoken" (Romans 4:18). Directly implied in this verse is that inheriting the huge promises of God that shake the world require that we first gain a

---

[6] Martin Buber, *I and Thou* (United States of America: Charles Scribner's Sons, 1970), p. 9. The line above is taken from Walter Kaufmann's prologue to this book. He begins the thought above with, "The truth is too complex and frightening."

major victory over natural thinking and logic. Siding with faith over logic puts the promises of God (our destinies) within reach.

Brain, Bow Down

The Western mind wants to make sense of everything, but clearly, by way of the gospels, this luxury of human reasoning is simply not available. I feel like I often dilute truth with my reasoning while it is the demand of ultimate truth that we allow our thinking to get challenged and changed by the Word. When Jesus is saying, "Whatever you ask of the Father in My name He may give to you" (John 15:16) then that is a true statement. End of story. No discussion. No excuses. No reasoning that will water this down to mean less than "whatever" implies. My experience of it doesn't determine its truth. It is only as I receive it as truth that it can actually become my experience. Receiving truth with biblical faith means that I am actually expecting it to be or become a reality to me in my life. It is mine to experience.

Did Pentecost make sense? Is Jesus' seeker-brutal service in John 6 logical? No. They both offend the mind, because they have to. The Holy Spirit will confront our reasoning and He wants to know who or what we'll side with as push comes to shove. Stumbling blocks and roadblocks look like brains on our narrow way into kingdom life and thinking. Testing is part of the spiritual life. For the religious and cerebral alike there will be a showdown between our intellect and the move of the Holy Ghost. We will be invited to move into the realms of power and authority, *true* riches, through a door that is marked "Faith" as you choose to become "certain of what you cannot see." Or we have the option of settling for good theology so that we can explain to others exactly what and why we believe what we do. Peter didn't understand Jesus message in John 6, but he knew that life was coming from Jesus and there was nowhere else to go (v. 68).

Fools Get Wisdom

The first gift of the Spirit listed is wisdom, and I believe this is so because living by the unseen will cause us to walk the line of foolishness. Kingdom authority is hidden from the wise by the world's standards. As a twist of insult, we are told that it is God's good pleasure to fix the spiritual life as such. It's a bit frustrating, isn't it? We may be good at quoting 2 Corinthians 5:7 when we're clearly without control in a particular situation after we've tried our best at the helm, but to live by faith and not by sight means that we are primarily living by a Presence from a realm that is concealed from most. It means that both what He has said and is saying in the present moment are to be truer than the evidence and facts of what is seen.

My internal GPS may direct me in a straight line over Mt. Rainier or across Lake Washington and He can simply not be corrected. Should we ever turn to God and say, "That's impossible!" It's in these moments that our faith is on trial. Will I side with God or with reasoning? What He is saying to us will only make sense to those who are living in their spirit, valuing the unseen over and above the natural circumstances. "A natural man does not accept the things of the Spirit of God, for they are foolishness to him; and he cannot understand them, because they are spiritually appraised" (1 Corinthians 2:14).

When we felt that we were first to open a free storefront venue in Seattle we knew that faith was required because free venues don't generate income. Following God in faith sounded great on paper, but at the beginning of the month we would still be required to have $2,400. So, we felt like we were supposed to open a free venue. Logic says, "That's impossible to sustain because you won't be able to pay rent." Living in faith, which is by definition being sure of what you hope for, says, "I know the funds will be there."

It is important to note that when we experience what feels like failure after a leap of faith, we cannot afford to begin to play it safe or come to conclusions about faith that are less than what God has defined it as. I need to learn what I can, throw everything else into the cupboard of mystery and continue to live recklessly obedient to the One who says, "I have given you authority to tread...over all the power of the enemy, and nothing will injure you" (Luke 10:19). If we risk and do not experience the result we wanted we approach a very crucial fork in the road where we can either choose to continue in faith or allow our disappointment to create a theology of faith that insulates us from future failure. Disappointments that lead us to blame God or become offended (how He "didn't come through for us") will surely put out of reach the abundant life He extends to us.

A Bout with Doubt

The main obstacle to walking in power and the anointed life that is extended to us is our unbelief. The words and promises of God often get shelved by disappointment and unanswered questions. We suffer loss and may subconsciously cease to accept these truths. If my circumstances disagree with or are in conflict with what God has said, then it is I who must contend with my natural reality until it conforms to the words of Jesus. He has said that "nothing will by any means harm me" (Luke 10:19), and so if I become sick or harmed in any way this does not give me rights to bring His word into question, decrease my expectation, or lower the Word to the level of my experience. We are to rise in this opportunity and demand that our lives and visible reality begin to line up with His Word.

Faith has to be tested (James 1:3) and this usually means that what we believe will come under fire and conflict. What we believe will appear to be false if we're living by sight alone. Just as Abraham took on his new name which contradicted his life (he was not, in fact, the father of a multitude...yet), we will be lead into circumstances that defy logic and reasoning where we will be invited to live by what we are sure we are hoping for and confident of what we cannot see (Heb. 11:1) or understand. This is the threshold of faith. This is the portal into another world (if you'll let me use some eerie language). This is entrance into a realm where God can trust us.

Co-laboring with God

While it is completely true that all authority and power and dominion belong to God, it is also true that He has freely given authority, power and dominion to us, the people who carry His name and are assigned to carry out His will on the earth—bringing life, health, salvation and deliverance. I used to have the impression that the Christian or minister's job was to be one who cries out to God to do miraculous stuff. However, He tells us to go do it, to bring the kingdom. This is what He has equipped us for. One instance stands out to me in the gospels where we are to ask God for something. We are to ask Him to send out laborers into the harvest. God is aching for people to be active in the harvest. In this Matthew 9 and 10 context Jesus sends His disciples, those who were just told to pray for workers, into the harvest to proclaim the kingdom of God and heal the sick and deliver those bound by demons. God is longing for believers to believe that what He has given us—power and authority—is ours to use. I feel Him longing for me to put them to use setting people free as we declare and demonstrate His kingdom and His reality, proving it to be true and truly good news.

Kingdom authority belongs to believers. "What I have I give to you", said Peter to the lame man prior to healing his legs as the power of God rushed into the man's feet and ankles giving them strength. Coming into this revelation and actually believing that we have kingdom authority as sons and daughters of the King is what Jesus was whipped and beaten for. His blood and death were for our sins and His beating was for our healing, according to Isaiah 53:5. "By His stripes you were healed." What I failed to see about the life of Jesus for so many years was that He was just as concerned with healing as He was the forgiveness of sins. Sickness in our bodies is a valid parallel to what sin is to our spirits, and Jesus often dealt with sin and sickness in the same move (Mt. 9:6).

The Co-mission of God

Revelation 5:10 reveals a startling truth about the nature, gift and responsibility of redeemed humanity. "You have made them to be a kingdom and priests to our God; and they will reign upon the earth." This means, just as it says, that God Himself has fashioned us (all who have been cleansed and "purchased" by the death of Jesus) to be kings, which implies that we have royal power, kingship, dominion and rule. And He has also fashioned and made us priests to our God; and we will reign on the earth. Once again, "reign" means to be king, and to exercise kingly power. Metaphorically, it means to exercise highest influence or control.

During the ministry years of Jesus there were a few markers of His way of life that caused people to stop in awe and wonder. His manifested and recognized authority was a key component that He modeled for normal Christianity. When people saw what Jesus did "they were awestruck, and glorified God, who had given such authority to men" (Matthew 9:8). People are still seeing what Jesus does through His church. They are glorifying God, who has given such authority to believers. The people in Matthew 9 recognized His authority because He had just brought healing to a paralyzed man. Jesus demonstrated the goodness and will of God through physical healing, and He is still longing to show His will and goodness as we move in the authority He has given us to cause praise to rise to God. People who follow Jesus' model of life are supposed to heal the sick just as Jesus Himself did.

4

AUTHORITY TO HEAL THE SICK

Jesus invited people to allow the miracles to verify the truth of his message and we must be able to do the same.

A Toddler's Revelation

When my son was two he was beating up on a passenger in the back seat of our car. We encouraged him to be nice and to be like Jesus. Immediately he put his hand out toward the pummeled passenger and said, "Be healed". It had taken him mere months to come to a conclusion that I didn't reach for thirty years—to be like Jesus is to heal people.

Invite anyone to read the gospels and have them tell you what they noticed about the life of Jesus and they would all mention how He healed people. The Christian life is not all about healing people. But because Jesus gave healing so much attention it must be an "ability" that is of great importance to me. For me, the confusion that had surrounded this gift landed me in a clouded state regarding this key marker of Jesus' life and ministry that we were always intended to walk in. The way I see it now: I'm a Christian, so, obviously, healing people is a normal part of my life.

Getting it Right

My experience with death and disease is limited, but I'm convinced that no one has to have prolonged exposure to such things before coming to the conclusion that it is horrible. Looking into the eyes of someone whose body is being eaten by cancer is crushing. "Disease" means that something is *wrong* in the body. Jesus took on human flesh in order to make things *right*. Peace is the state of things as they should be. He came preaching peace and told His disciples to let their peace rest on people and places as they went out. Jesus came to reveal the nature of God and bring heaven's standard to earth. Desiring or *willing* that someone would be ill flows *against* the ministry of Jesus and contradicts the revealed nature of God that Jesus embodied.

When I come alongside the suffering, and as I battle for my wife who has struggled with crippling migraines for 14 years, I feel angry. There is a holy boiling within me for justice. My anger is fuel for my pursuit of holiness and for the fullness of God's nature to rest on me. We all know that if Jesus were in the room, healing would happen in an instant. I know I am destined to be like Jesus because I carry the name Christian.

Paradigm Under Pressure

Although I followed Jesus and He was always healing people, I don't think I even had a paradigm for healing for the first 30 years of my life. I heard of people getting healed but it was so random and mysterious. I had no category to put it in. Healing was so unpredictable. My uncle had his leg lengthened and back healed by the power of God. When I was a kid, my youth pastor's daughter was healed of autism. Yet my brother, a man serving God, had a son born with severe heart issues. Why certain people got healed and others didn't usually leads most to assume that God's just going to do what God's going to do.

Jesus put my paradigm in a vice. As I welcomed the revealed nature of Jesus in regards to healing I had to release all my questions. I could not afford to hold God hostage with my questions or refuse to obey because I didn't understand something. Because He healed everyone who came to Him, this told me something very critical about His nature and will.

The Track Record

Follow me through a handful of verses that detail the ministry of Jesus. Jesus did not just heal *some* people. He healed *everyone* who came to Him in need of healing. He modeled a lifestyle that brought physical healing to everyone who came to Him needing a miracle. We may speculate otherwise, but the gospels tell of His all-inclusive habit of healing. Everyone who came to Him got healed. Say it aloud: Everyone.

At the very beginning of the ministry of Jesus he "was going throughout all Galilee, teaching in their synagogues and proclaiming the gospel of the kingdom, and healing every kind of disease and every kind of sickness among the people" (Matthew. 4:23).

"The news about Him spread throughout all Syria; and they brought to Him all who were ill, those suffering with various diseases and pains, demoniacs, epileptics, paralytics; and He healed them" (Matthew 4:24).

"When evening came, they brought to Him many who were demon-possessed; and He cast out the spirits with a word, and healed all who were ill" (Matthew 8:16).

"Jesus was going through all the cities and villages, teaching in their synagogues and proclaiming the gospel of the kingdom, and healing every kind of disease and every kind of sickness" (Matthew 9:35). This passage demonstrates that it was the habit and practice of Jesus, and the nature of His ministry, to demonstrate the reality of the gospel (the good news; the kingdom of God) by healing everyone wherever He went. Every kind of disease and sickness was obliterated. Although this is but one passage that says that Jesus was healing everyone, it clearly shows that this manner of healing ministry was done with startling frequency. This all-inclusive healing was taking place in every city and village. "*All* the cities and villages." "*Every* kind of disease and *every* kind of sickness." Think of it. This is the nature of God as revealed by Jesus. He went through every city and village and healed everyone who had need of healing.

"But Jesus, aware of this, withdrew from there. Many followed Him, and He healed them all" (Matthew 12:15).

"When He went ashore, He saw a large crowd, and felt compassion for them and healed their sick" (Mt. 14:14).

"And large crowds came to Him, bringing with them those who were lame, crippled, blind, mute, and many others, and they laid them down at His feet; and He healed them" (Matthew 15:30).

"When Jesus had finished these words, He departed from Galilee and came into the region of Judea beyond the Jordan; and large crowds followed Him, and He healed them there" (Matthew 19:1, 2).

"While the sun was setting, all those who had any who were sick with various diseases brought them to Him; and laying His hands on each one of them, He was healing them" (Luke 4:40).

"Jesus came down with them and stood on a level place; and there was a large crowd of His disciples, and a great throng of people from all Judea and Jerusalem and the coastal region of Tyre and Sidon, who had come to hear Him and to be healed of their diseases; and those who were troubled with unclean spirits were being cured. And all the people were trying to touch Him, for power was coming from Him and healing them all" (Luke 6:17-19).

"But the crowds were aware of this and followed Him; and welcoming them, He began speaking to them about the kingdom of God and curing those who had need of healing" (Luke 9:11).

Gospel Conclusions About Healing

Jesus never *will*-ed anyone to remain in physical pain. Though this may not be our experience with God, it is the revealed nature of God in Jesus. Healing is the nature of God. It is always His will and desire and choice to heal. Yet this is where the important connection has to be made: all authority in heaven and on earth has been given to Jesus, and He has, in turn, given that authority to us (Mt. 10:1). The Body is to move with the power and authority and the rights that reside in the Head, Jesus. Being Jesus' hands and feet means we go places He would go, to the people He'd go to and we do what He would do, bringing healing to every sick and tormented person we encounter. After God had begun to highlight these "all" passages to me I became more and more baffled as to how I used to tolerate sickness around me. The accounts of Jesus healing everyone are so clear and frequent, yet I had for so long had my theology of healing rooted in solo, unclear passages like Paul's "thorn in the flesh".

How can it be that people who follow Jesus as their model for life could have a theology that is passive toward sickness? It is an abomination to the lifestyle of Jesus to say that God would ever cause sickness, will a disease for someone or bring death. What activity of Jesus could ever lead us to the conclusion that God would give someone cancer in order to bring Himself glory? Jesus lived violently against death and disease, never once giving it a place or purpose in His presence. He may indeed bring good out of a situation involving sickness, but in order to place God as the cause of that sickness, or conclude that it is persisting by His choice or will, one must ignore the life message of Jesus, who healed everyone...repeatedly.

God has put His power, authority, and anointing on us in order that His choice for everyone's complete wholeness becomes the experience of humanity. Everyone getting healed is no longer God's responsibility. He has made every provision for us to pick up where Jesus left off. This became one of the most important understandings for me to come into in regards to the healing ministry. It also proved to be one of the most difficult realities, initially, to accept and apply faith.

Traditional Sunday Service Re-Experienced

I have announced it on Sunday before: "If you don't experience miracles here, you don't have to believe what we're talking about." Miracles bring people to a place a decision, and amongst a Body of believers where there is no power or miracles it can rightly be debated whether or not this church is Christian. Being Christian is synonymous with being powerful. Remember, "Christian" means there is power and anointing. Professed common beliefs may earn the label Christian, but it does not infer a re-presentation of Jesus. Looking at us, the world is intended to see the nature and goodness of God. Often, that nature is seen when God stretches out His hand through you to heal the sick, release miracles and the evidence that God is alive and more powerful and loving than the darkness of any inner city or inner life.

Many have come to our church and received physical healing in their first visit. God encounters them in worship or through someone's prayer and legs have been lengthened, back pain gone, digestive issues cured, and deaf ears opened. On one of her first Sundays in Church of the Undignified, a woman received prayer for her uneven legs that had caused her much pain. Her leg was told to grow out in Jesus' name and it did! She was able to go home and take the hem out of all the pant legs that had been sewn up so they wouldn't get stepped on. Behold, the power of God!

We had a youth group visit us one summer and we spoke to them a little about healing during a devotional time. Youth are amazing because they expect it to happen just as they have been told. Their capacity for faith has not yet been buried under disappointment and logic. When we proceeded into a time of experience and demonstration we all gathered around a young girl who was on crutches with a wounded knee. I invited one of the other youths present to go ahead and speak to the knee and tell it what you want it to do. "You have authority." I think she meant to tell the pain to leave but instead she said, "Knee, leave in Jesus' name." I've always been glad that God can interpret the meaning of our prayers and actions. The knee was healed in that moment in front of us all and we watched the girl squat low and then stand up straight. When we left the house, she walked up the stairs holding the crutches in one hand.

When healing is released through a believer we are not so much praying for the healing as we are releasing healing. We mostly relate prayer to asking God to do something. But if we look at prayer at a more general level as being in communication with God, then we can say that we are in prayer (as we are to be constantly) as we release healing, His kingdom and His will in a situation.

Because the Christian life is one of intimacy with our Heavenly Father, our operation in His gifts runs alongside our love for the Father and His love for people. As we reign with Him here on earth and establish His kingdom, the standard of heaven brought on earth, we are invited to enjoy His love and see the fruit that flows from this union (John 15:5, 10). Power for healing is to be an overflow of our love relationship with God and our Christlike compassion for the sick and tormented.

The Seen, Felt, Marvel-ous Gospel

Christianity is a lifestyle that is to be demonstrated and shown. It is a faith that requires both word of explanation and power. Without power it is not the gospel (1 Cor. 4:20). Without signs and wonders the gospel is not fully being proclaimed (Romans 15:19). It is the demonstration of this good news and the reality of God and His kingdom that gives opportunity for faith to arise, because our faith was always intended to rest on the power of God (1 Corinthians 2:4). Christianity across the globe is getting back to our foundational assignment in Matthew 10:8. We, like Elijah, are once again announcing, "The God who answers by fire, He is God" (1 Kings 18:24). Let me prove it! "Heal those who are sick, and say to them, 'The kingdom of God has come near to you'" (Luke 10:9). Jesus invited the people to allow the miracles to verify the truth of His message and we must be able to do the same.

The Fuel for Power

Power flows from our faith but it is also held up by our uncertainty. Believing that we actually are a new creation, co-heirs with Christ, seated in heavenly places with Him, having authority over all sickness and all the power of the enemy, etc. will drastically alter what we expect to occur around us. Hunger for the things of God, expectation, and pursuit of the kingdom and His righteousness are some of the sparks that ignite the fuel that is God's holy presence that ever-surrounds us.

There's No Gospel in Sympathy

As Church of the Undignified grew out of a missional service project I had to make the transition from missionary to pastor. I moved from sowing into the lives of unbelievers to giving my time and attention mostly to believers that were becoming part of a growing family. Delving into pastoral ministry I did what I knew to do—listen well, give counsel, pray and encourage. I was unfulfilled in my role in other people's lives, as I wanted to really make a difference. I began to realize that my idea of comfort was not found is Scripture. I equated comfort with listening, pity, consolation, and making sure they knew I felt bad for them in their misfortune or horrible circumstances. The aforementioned is more a job description of sympathy than it is of compassion or comfort.

Our typical understanding of the word "sympathy" is not used in the Bible. I believe this is because it is an entirely worldly way of comfort. It is not a bad thing to do; it is simply a presence and gesture that is without power. Comfort and compassion are actions founded in the nature of God and when they are applied, it lifts (immediately or eventually) people out of their funk, their pain, and their depression. Being a comforter, the name and job description of the Holy Spirit, means that we will draw near to people, encourage them and lead them into truth and reality. It will be administered in love, tenderness, great patience and great power because the source will be heaven and not our own ability to simply "offer an ear". This is not to downplay the power of giving our attention and listening ear, this is simply pointed so that we may be sure to partner with heaven to bring power to hopeless circumstances. Again, the model is Jesus. Though He drew near as a friend to those in need, He was not offering friendship for their consolation. He offered power, healing and life. He didn't invited Mary and Martha to cry on Him when their brother, Lazarus, died. *Jesus* cried and then He brought the dead man out of his grave.

Jesus never applied bandages but went to the actual problem. When someone is sick or diseased, what is the real need? The real problem is not the need for company or someone to cry with. The real problem is cancer or a broken leg. Pain is the reason we are where we are, gathered in a hospital as a family. Of course we celebrate and allow the nurturing development of family and friendships, seeing a family or the Body become more and more one. But we must not opt out of our commissioning to bring the power for the impossible and destroy the works of the devil or bring heaven's standard to tragic moments.

Paul informs us that we are to mourn with those who mourn. This, too, is an absolute requirement. What I am emphasizing is our need to venture into the realm of the impossible. We obey what Jesus has sent us and empowered us to do without using Paul's instruction as a loophole to remove ourselves from responsibility to walk in the miraculous.

I have been beside the hospital beds of those being kept alive by machines. I have stood over corpses with other believers and we know what we're there for. We may be sympathetic with the family and mourn with them, but my responsibility in those moments as one who hosts the life of God is to call down heaven, release God's kingdom and will and destroy death and disease. God's will is "on earth as it is in heaven" (Mt. 6:10). No one is sick or dying in heaven![7]

Straight Up Sent

There is not much need for an interpretation of Luke 9:1-2. The expectation of the disciples was pretty straightforward. "And He called the twelve together, and gave them power and authority over all the demons and to heal diseases. And He sent them to proclaim the kingdom of God and to perform healing." This was Professor Jesus' Bible School and Seminary. I imagine Jesus following up this 20-second pep talk saying, "Alright. Good talk. You guys are awesome. Go, get 'em!" The disciples don't even ask questions. "Departing, they began going throughout the villages, preaching the gospel and healing everywhere" (v. 6). Christians are supposed to heal people of diseases.

Though I had believed for a long time that healing was God's

---

[7] While we do see the elderly die around us, we never see Jesus explaining that it was someone's "time" to die. I don't believe we have permission to make those judgments either. We are to heal the sick and raise the dead (Mt. 10:8).

responsibility, the words of Jesus clearly state otherwise. Responsibility for healing and miracles in our world rests on the shoulders on the one(s) who have authority and power to perform them. Jesus had power and authority to perform miracles, and He gave His disciples power and authority to perform miracles.

Just for the Original 12?

Some of the Great Commission's details are found in the original sending. The disciples were instructed to make disciples in every nation, "teaching them to observe all that I commanded you" (Matthew 28:20). A key part of what the disciples had been commanded to do was to heal the sick, raise the dead and cast out demons (Mt. 10:8). And they were to pass these instructions on to every single person who would believe and follow Jesus.

How Jesus "Saved"

God has entrusted His followers, the believers, with His Spirit and the mission of extending His salvation to the world. The New Testament word for being "saved" (sozo) also carries the elements of being healed and delivered. His salvation touches every part of the human being. Often when people received physical healing from Jesus it is said that they were sozo-ed. "For she thought, 'If I just touch His garments, I will get well'" (Mark 5:28). The word "sozo" is used here and it is translated "get well". His salvation contains physical healing, as well as the forgiveness of sin. Jesus' desire to see people "saved" meant that people would encounter

His healing power, saving power, forgiving power and delivering power. God's will is for His complete peace to rest on people. The kingdom of heaven is to come upon people and cause things to be as they ought to be. This is justice and *right*eousness.

Physical healing is not the main point. People who are obediently praying for the sick know that it is not the main point. In the gospels, healing is simply one of God's obvious manners of revealing His nature, His will, demonstrating His goodness and His kingdom, and meeting people in their pain and cry for relief and "saving".

There are many experiences that have caused us to become uncertain or unconvinced regarding the gift and ministry of healing. There have been many abuses and a lot of blame. It is not my goal to address the many questions that arise about the ministry of healing. It is my passion to pursue and uncover this aspect of Christ's life that had been in the dark corners of my Bible and life. So, how do we get started in healing the sick? Let's turn to that subject now.

5
FUELING FAITH

If Jesus said I had authority then I did.
What was missing was belief, not answers to my questions.

Overcoming Fear

When I was just coming into the practice of extending healing to others I remember walking over to Safeway as I did frequently, and I would be gearing myself up. "I'm not going to back down or chicken out!" It took me awhile to learn that these encounters usually occur naturally and are to flow out of a place of love and rest. When beginning, since the activity of healing prayer is so foreign to both parties, we often need to accept the element of awkwardness that tends to accompany our following of Jesus' model. People will give me weird looks, bluntly say "no", or may even insult me. But obedience has no fear of rejection. Love, when perfected, gets rid of any and every kind of fear (1 John 4:18). Approaching people with loving concern usually is met with gratitude and they can feel your love. If they happen to get healed then they not only feel our love but they get to encounter the power of God's love, too.

Once I believed that God wanted me to go about relieving people of pain in His name, I encountered an obstacle called The Fear of Man. Fear (or "timidity") is a spirit (2 Tim. 1:7) and this demon is set on keeping people from having a transforming affect on their neighborhoods. Since there is no fear in Love there should be no fear in any believer. Being a person who keeps to himself most naturally, it was a real stretch to offer healing prayer to strangers. My blood would be pumping, heart racing and I would try to muster enough nerve to step up to an impossibility and invite Holy Spirit to come in His love and power.

Getting Started

Unfortunately, many of us do not have an interest in healing until we have a close friend or relative who is sick or dying. Trying to develop a theology of healing while a loved one is fighting for his or her life is not ideal timing. Because gifts are abilities that need to be developed, trying to tap into an unknown gift when we suddenly find ourselves in a crisis often leads to false conclusions about the gift, the nature of God and the will God. Being surrounded by suffering people our interest in healing is a "now" need. But getting out the door, our tight schedules and outside ourselves to pray for the sick or afflicted that we encounter every week exposes obstacles. The common obstacles to living naturally supernatural are fear and unbelief.

"Can *I* heal?"

"Does God want to now?"

"What if nothing happens?"

"I'll look like an idiot, or a fanatic!"

"I really don't think anything will happen."

Attempting to operate in the gift of healing initially is usually more about *our* spiritual development and relationship with God than it is about whether or not the person we pray for gets healed. Yet the author of our faith unmistakably modeled healing for everyone who came to Him. And for the sake of our cities, this is the standard we thirst for.

Coming Up Short

Walking to the post office one day I came by a woman near a gas station who was in a wheelchair. Once she had my attention she showed me the coins in her hand and asked if I would go into the gas station's market and buy her the beer she wanted. Although a bit conflicted, I agreed to help her, convinced that I was meeting here in her present need. She was not allowed in the store and the beer was the bridge that allowed me access into her life and need.

She cracked the can open, and as the beer entered her body so did some natural peace. I knelt next to her and she began to tell me her story. She had been in an abusive relationship, and her man actually shot her in the leg. The wound was so severe that the right leg had to be amputated. So now she sits in this chair, missing a leg and half of her upper body is almost completely paralyzed. She admitted to treating the pain with substances. Her tears revealed the obvious fact that she was without hope and not proud of her plight.

I did my best to relay how God saw her as I told her how amazing and beautiful she was. She let me pray for the healing of her paralysis, though there didn't seem to be any improvement in the moment. What she really wanted was a pillow. The stump of her leg was in pain as the weight of her body pressed it hard into the seat of the wheelchair. I walked two blocks back to my home, found a nice, fancy pillow and gave it to her. She wanted help positioning it just right, so she pulled up her dress to expose what remained of her leg. She asked me to lift of the "leg" and put the pillow underneath. The smell was horrible. I put my hand under her leg and it was instantly wet with sweat and what was likely urine, judging by the odor. I slid the pillow under her and she was comforted and thankful.

Though I was able to comfort her to an extent, I feel that my actions as someone who is supposed to re-present Jesus fell drastically short. When I left here she was still paralyzed on half her upper body and she still had just one leg. Had *Jesus* knelt next to her wheel, she would have stood up on two legs, been lost in praise and wonder, and her tears would have turned to joy.

Stretching Toward the Standard

What was clearly of importance to Jesus must be important to me. He healed and delivered afflicted people and commissioned His disciples to also go "heal the sick, raise the dead, cleanse the lepers, cast out demons" (Matthew 10:8). The Christianity that will bring heaven's standard to earth will move in great power. We received power when the Holy Spirit came upon us and the kingdom of God is not in word but in power (1 Cor. 4:20).

Here's the standard of the Christian life as it's been intended: whoever wants healing or breakthrough will get it when we're around. That's the model we have in Jesus. That's what we've been equipped for. Alcoholics will be delivered, their livers healed, hope restored. But it seems that this gospel, the good news Jesus extended, has been explained too well while His standard has been buried under our disappointments, unbelief and lack of experience.

I began to understand that my experience (or lack of it) in the ministry of healing and deliverance did not cause His words to be rewritten. If He says I have authority then I do. My mind was swimming when I first began to entertain the thought that He wanted to heal people through me, His Spirit moving within and through me. Talking to God out loud as I drove over the Ballard Bridge one day, I questioned Him excitedly and with joy. "Really? Are You going to heal people through me? Really? Really?!" With each question He would answer, "I give you authority." It didn't matter if the question or statement I uttered fit that reply. The words "I give you authority" just continued to resound in my spirit. I was beginning to understand His heart. If He said I had authority then I did. What was missing was belief, not answers to my questions.

Everyone's Gift of Healing

Approaching the gift of healing believers will often remember Paul's words more than they will Jesus' words. Does everyone have the gift of healing? In 1 Corinthians 12 Paul goes over the nine gifts of the Spirit and then begins to explain that not everyone has the same gifts. "All do not have gifts of healing, do they?" (12:30). It is my understanding that Paul is describing what is taking place in a believer's meeting. As the Spirit is moving in a meeting someone may be used to heal that "Sunday", another may have a prophetic word, another an interpretation to a message that was spoken in an unknown language.

However we interpret 1 Corinthians 12, we must allow what Jesus has said to help us interpret what Paul is saying. Jesus has directly instructed us to heal the sick, so regardless of what Paul may be talking about, we are all still supposed to heal the sick. Yes, actually heal the sick, the diseased, the dying, the injured, the demonized and the dead. Jesus would not send us out to heal the sick and not give us the ability to do so. Since He has told us to do it, this means that it is possible for us to do it.

We usually conclude that someone has the gift of healing because people get healed when he or she prays for others. I believe this approach has contributed to the dying out of this ministry. This gift is available to every believer because every believer has the Holy

Spirit within. Within the Spirit are the gifts of the Spirit. The moment we receive Jesus, Holy Spirit sets up shop within us, and every good thing, fruit and gift is now available to us. It is faith that makes what's available accessible (Rom. 5:2). We receive all of the Holy Spirit, not just parts of His nature and power. He's *all* in there! Putting the gift to work with expectation allows that gift to mature.

How the Gift of Healing is Developed

There is often a passive approach to the gifts of the Spirit surmising that if God wants to give me a gift then He will. I used to think I was keeping myself centered by saying that I would just pursue God and not His gifts. But that's not the way He set it up.

Paul instructs us that we are to earnestly and lustfully desire the spiritual gifts (1 Cor. 14:1). We are supposed to seek not just the One above but also the "things" above and to set our mind on these things (Col. 3:1-2). God wants us desiring the things of heaven and the lifestyle of Jesus in order that we may contribute to the transformation of our world. This is seeking first His kingdom and His righteousness. In His kingdom there is no sickness and with His righteousness fully formed in us we will eradicate all the works of the enemy around us. We will put an end to disease, death and the demonic that oppresses the people around us.

We pray and cry out and hunger for the gifts of the Spirit to be manifest in our lives. We are to cry out for the gifts in our secret place and look for the answer to these prayers as we go out. We have this assurance: if we ask anything in accordance with His will we know that we have what we asked for (1 John 5:14-15). It is faith that takes this at face value. God has asked us to heal the sick so it is obviously deduced that He wants us to heal the sick. So, when we ask to be able to heal the sick we are praying in line with His will for our lives. God loves it when we pray in line with His desires for us, when we seek to unwrap the gifts that He has carefully and intentionally designed for us. When we walk in these amazing gifts it will lead to the kingdom come. The pursuit of these gifts is a hungering for His kingdom and righteousness.

We also pursue the healing gift by attempting to move in the gifting. It is in this exercise and lifestyle that the gifts are formed in us along with all the virtues and fruits of the Spirit being sharpened. The writer of Hebrews gives us these insightful words on the process of maturity: "For everyone who partakes only of milk is not accustomed to the word of righteousness, for he is an infant. But solid food is for the mature, who because of practice have their senses trained to discern good and evil" (Hebrews 5:13-14). "Practice", or it is sometimes translated "constant use", is a key factor in maturity and Christlikeness. And we will likely find that the sick are getting healed with greater frequency when we consistently pray for the sick. The word "practice" here is also defined in greater detailed as

1) a habit whether of body or mind
2) a power acquired by custom, practice, use[8]

It helped me to view the gifts of God as seeds within me. The ability to have them is there but it often takes the fuel of faith and

[8] http://www.blueletterbible.org/lang/lexicon/lexicon.cfm?Strongs=G1838&t=NASB

expectation mixed with a persistence and pressing in that acts as water and healthy soil to these kingdom seeds. It happens different for everyone because we are talking about a relationship with God, so it does little good to compare details of how we obtain gifts. I can't say, "Do this and it will happen for you because that is what happened for me." Instead, we invite each other and spur each other on to discover together the different aspects of the move of the Spirit, the love of God and how we are experiencing "your kingdom come, on earth as it is in heaven."

A Key Common Denominator

Over the course of the last century there have been many individuals who have lived with great authority and they exercised it over demons and diseases. All of them lived with the revelation and conviction that sickness was from the devil and that all healing had already been paid for, just as all forgiveness had already been paid for.

Doing the Word

Jesus presented many interesting and dynamic tensions, and one of these is the issue surrounding proofs or signs. He came down on people who asked for signs, yet also invited the unbelieving to believe because of the miracles He was doing. Jesus used miracles, signs and wonders to prove His authenticity. "So that you may know that the Son of Man has authority on earth to forgive sins, stand up and walk" (Mt. 9:6). People will again know that Jesus has power on earth to forgive sins because of the miracles and healings that occur at the hands of His followers, believers.

"Jesus the Nazarene, a man attested to you by God with miracles and wonders and signs which God performed through Him in your midst" (Acts 2:22). Miracles proved what kind of person Jesus was. He was a human whom God worked through powerfully. We, too, are intended to be people who are proven to be authentically of God by the miracles that take place when we are around.

Humiliated and Loving It!

There have been many people that have been healed and I do not remember the story or the person, but one encounter that is most lodged in my memory is one in which seemingly nothing happened. I went into a busy coffee shop, like you do in the great Northwest, and noticed a gal in a huge foot brace. I got my drink and stopped by her table and inquired about the injury. Even though she and her friend were perplexed by my offer to give healing prayer they consented anyway. I put my hand on her ankle, said a brief command over the ailing leg and then looked back up at the couple. They looked at me as if, to quote A Christmas Story, I had lobsters crawling out of my ears. I left that shop and the most overwhelming sense of joy came over me. So many other times I had found myself in opportunities like that where I could give God a platform to move and show His glory, yet I would bow out in fear. This time I won out. I was victorious. I stepped out, not caring about being awkward, embarrassed or making people feel uncomfortable. I was obedient to my call and I attempted in faith to make manifest the love and power of God. And God poured joy out in my heart and all over my face as a result. I felt that a dagger had been thrust into my flesh (my sinful, self-centered nature) as I did not submit to the demon of fear but dealt my pride another major blow.

Win-Win

I soon discovered the win-win scenario that is presented when we step out to heal strangers in public. Either more of your flesh dies as you suffer some humiliation or someone experiences loving concern or gets healed. Yet more than the healing itself people always get a love encounter. A seed of the kingdom is planted within them. A person has engaged someone from the kingdom of His Son and it will have some effect. They now know that there are people who walk with an expectation and in an experience of God that is current, miraculous, powerful and is able to meet any need. They have a faith encounter as well as a love encounter. These virtues are powerfully influential. They change atmospheres, deliver hope, release joy and expectation. People will often at least thank you for caring for them and showing concern. The worst thing that can happen is that you are totally humiliated as they reject you and your offer to heal or pray for them. And in this "worst" scenario, you grow by leaps and bounds in the Spirit and in your faith. We grow in the favor of God also as we demonstrate to Him that we are moved by what His desires are and not by the opinions and praises of others.

Anointed Ones

It is this call into the normal, miraculous life that gives explanation to our "Christian" title. "Christ" means "anointed one" and we are "anointed ones". We have been smeared with the very presence of God and equipped for greatness, miracles and to powerfully demonstrate who God is and what He's like. Jesus was "anointed with the Holy Spirit and with power, and he went around doing good, healing all who were oppressed by the devil for God was with Him" (Acts 10:38). This verse not only describes the life of Jesus but our lives as well. We've been blessed and blasted with the Holy Spirit without measure (John 3:34), with power, and we've been assigned to go around and heal everyone oppressed by the devil. This is called "doing good". This activity is the simple byproduct of agreeing with God and releasing His presence that fills us. People get healed because God is with us and because we actually expect healing and deliverance to occur. We boil with expectation. That is what faith for a healing looks like.

6

THE PATH TO MORE

While God is present to all, there is a measure of His presence and gifting that is unattainable for people who are not all in...or fallout along the way. Hunger brings us in, faith gives us the ability to endure and supernatural hope keeps discouragement away.

First Exposures

Hunger will take you strange places. I was in college the first time I attended a conference of the "charismatic" type. It was a sight to behold. People were laughing hysterically, there were unknown sounds and a guy I knew claimed he was punched in the stomach when he went up for prayer. During the service a guy was on stage explaining, "It's clear that God is in the room. If you are not feeling Him, perhaps there is some sin in your life." I was not feeling God. And I would learn later that "feeling" Him is not the primary way I notice His presence or activity. The only thing I was aware of was this new church environment hosting new-to-me behavior. I had never seen anything like it before.

The next time I stepped into a meeting with similar activity I was a Seattle missionary and I was hungry. In college I was curious. But this time I was aware of my need for more of God and the Holy Spirit's activity in my life and ministry. The worship team was lead by a Brazilian team whose leader had been healed of Down's Syndrome. I heard incredible testimonies of God's miraculous move around the globe and I did my best to receive all that was going forth from the stage. Yet still I was struggling. The environment was beyond my comfort and familiarity, but I now believe that the resistance within me was due to a religious spirit in me. I began to notice later, in the Gospels, that it was the religious spirit that blinded people from acknowledging the miracles that were occurring in front of their eyes and allowing that divine activity to bring them to a place of praise.

The Pharisees, who were the religious experts, witnessed a man's withered hand grow out and be restored to normal right in front of them! They responded not with praise and amazement but with plans as to how they might destroy Jesus. Aware of their planning, Jesus took off. And every single one of the many that followed Him got healed (Matthew 12:9-15). The religious nature will often revolt against the unconventional and miss the move of God even when it taps them on the nose. But those who follow Him experience miracles.

Attending an unconventional meeting where the unpredictable wind of the Spirit blew caused my religious spirit to be put under the knife. I was so uncomfortable in those meetings. So much strange activity and language was occurring around me and I was barely able to believe the testimonies that I heard. But Abbi and I would return to our car each day as we left the conference and I would tell God, "I want more of you. I want to see miracles. And if I can get breakthrough here then I'll keep coming back."

Judging Intimacy

Several years later I remember having a conversation with a very bright young man who was in the same battle with the religious spirit that I had gained some victory over. He was questioning many of the things we were doing as a church, particularly how we worship. I suppose if you call a church "Church of the Undignified", the worship will begin to look absurd. "Undignified" was the term David used to describe his own dance of praise to God as he celebrated before Him wearing nothing but a thin ephod. His celebration earned him the ridicule of even his wife, who lived allowing the opinions of others to determine her responses to God (2 Samuel 6:14-23).

Worship is one of the greatest forms of vulnerability and intimacy. Those who worship in spirit and truth will be stripped of all pretenses, religious routine and an awareness of others. Worshiping in spirit means, I believe, that we are more in His realm than we are our own. Our worship will be raw gratitude and adoration that flows from a grateful heart.

As I sat and listened to the young man talk about how some of our worship looks, I thought about how ridiculous it is to watch and judge the intimacy of others. Then this analogy came: Suppose you were out on a date with your spouse. You're sitting in a restaurant together and then glance over to see a man and a woman at another table. He is animated as he tells her how wonderful she is and what she means to him. She listens calmly as long as she can before she just erupts in tears and joy. As you see this, you lean across the table and whisper, "Do you think he means all that? Do you suppose she's pretending to cry?" Judging another person's intimacy with God is even more absurd. Can we know how God is touching a person? In a worship setting, why are we looking at someone else being intimate with God anyway? Trying to determine the authenticity of another relationship only poisons our own capacity for intimacy.

Freedom is offensive. Those who live free will always incur judgment and criticism from those who lack liberty. It was my immaturity, lack of freedom and limited experiences with the actual manifest presence of God that led me to question how others engaged God. While I still do not often "feel" God in times of great communal worship, I have learned to know how He is moving by how others are responding to Him, which brings me into a deeper place of praise.

Judging the intimacy and manifestations of others as they are before God will only set up a high standard of judgment on our own lives. The grace and judgments we issue to others create the guidelines for how grace and judgment is measures back to us

(Matthew 7:2). Since we set our own parameters and filters for how much grace lands on us, it makes the most sense to always assume others to be genuine. For this reason Jesus gives some good advice when He tells us to not judge at all. "Do not judge so that you will not be judged" (Matthew 7:1). Hear that. If we live assuming good of others we will live in the clear of any and all judgment. That has to be motivating.

Critical Barriers

The kingdom of God will remain out of reach to the religious and the skeptical. Unbelief will rob you of experiencing the power of God, yet it is the issue of judgment that keeps us in the natural and out of the realm of His kingdom, which is a spiritual arena. A critical spirit will live noticing the actions of others and it has been trained to question. We may think we are testing in order to prove something, but critical hearts simply create barriers against the One we long to encounter.

Even though I had been hungry for the more of God, it had been my criticism of others, or comparing myself to them, which kept the more of God out of my reach. Comparison is a fruit of judgment and those who are prone to comparison cannot be trusted with all God wants to give. Judgment is an indicator that someone is living more by sight than by faith. Living by faith, which is being sure of what you hope for and certain of what you cannot see (Hebrews 11:1), has its anchor in the spirit, on His kingdom and His righteousness. This perfect perspective will eventually bring us to such a place of freedom that we will lose all fear of pleasing or offending others as we pursue a life of reckless and powerful obedience.

The Path to More

One of the primary ways people enter into new realms of the Spirit is by getting around those who are experiencing higher realms of the Spirit than you. The religious spirit revolts against this path because that spirit is fed by pride. And pride will not admit that another person may be experiencing something greater than you are. Particularly for those who have been thoroughly educated and been practicing ministry for decades, it is a very humbling (humiliating) thing to come under the revelation that they have been missing something of great value. Honest, humble hunger will drive someone to not only crave God's presence but also the presence of those who are experiencing the life that they want. Paul even encouraged others to imitate him (1 Cor. 4:16; 11:1). Finding human beings who were living closer to the life of Jesus than I was rewarded me with what I was craving. It makes good sense that I could access more of God from His Body. There is also an impartation that can take place as others pray for us. Gifts of God can actually be activated in us when others lay their hands on us and release what they have (1 Tim. 1:6).

The Overriding Hunger

The more we are immersed in the life and activity of the Spirit, the more questions we will have. He is the one who leads us into all truth, and we will come under incredible, life-giving revelations. The questions and mystery that we are invited to live with are intended to bring us to deeper places of intimacy and trust. In our pursuit of the kingdom and righteousness of God in us and among us, many barriers will rise. But it will be faith and hunger that will beat down all obstacles that rise against our destiny to fully reflect His image and establish His kingdom on the earth.

It will be our faith and hunger for God that will allow us to hurdle obstacles and go beyond what is normal or acceptable in order to obtain and enjoy what is available. Our fixation is on the life of Jesus, who has demonstrated to mankind what it looks like for man to live in right relationship to God. If our gaze is on the people, we immediately lose sight of the goal—our lives being conformed to His.

When I began to really thirst for more of God I was welcomed into a Vineyard church. Abbi and I were in our first years ministering in Seattle and the darkness caused a stir in us, knowing that we had to have the power of God in order to effectively minister to the oppressed region we lived in. Becoming mentored by Rich and Rose Swetman, they taught us a lot about the gifts of the Spirit, deliverance and church life. My transition into life in the Spirit proved to be surprisingly unnatural.

Abbi and I were invited to a women's prayer meeting that the Vineyard held during a midweek lunch hour. We would go every week and I would sit there before God as the powerful women around me cried out in tongues for an hour. I felt a bit sidelined because I didn't have the gift of tongues but I knew God was powerfully at work among this group and I wanted to be around powerful people. If Paul had instructed others to follow him as he followed Christ, then it would be good idea for me to get around powerful people if I wanted to be powerful. I wanted the gifts of the Spirit so I hung around those who operated in the gifts. My hunger kept me going and my discomfort was kicked to backseat.

Sleep and Food are Optional

Hearing testimonies and learning what was available to me as a believer caused a growl of unreasonable hunger to emerge. I would wake in the night praying. I would get up early and just press in for all that God has for me, convinced that He wanted to give *everything* to me. The nature of my fasting turned from times of desperation to times of hunger for His presence. I fasted for nearness. I wanted more of His presence and more of His kingdom and His righteousness.

At a conference I heard Graham Cooke say that, "God is not available to the casual seeker." God says, "You will seek Me and find Me when you search for Me with all your heart" (Jer. 29:13). "With *all* your heart." While God is present to all, there is a measure of His presence and gifting that will be unattainable for people who are not all in. I was losing sleep and gaining momentum.

I'm 5'11" and weigh 150 pounds, so when I fast it can feel like I'm wasting away. It seems like others can be fine for days but I'll lose energy quickly because my body doesn't have much fat to burn through. During one three-week fast I dipped to 125 pounds. My body was waning yet my spirit was on fire. I would often be stirred as I recalled how fasting shaped Jesus, and this truth kept going through my mind: "And Jesus returned to Galilee in the power of the Spirit" (Luke 4:14). Miraculously, I felt fine and had enough energy to get through my days. I was motivated by God's presence and the power He had destined me to walk in.

I remember sitting at the kitchen table on the morning I would be breaking my fast. I had fasted for more of His presence and to get into greater levels of faith and authority. In front of me was a piece of warm banana bread with melting butter on it. A cup of coffee steamed next to it. And as delightful as it all was I said, "God, I just want more of you."

Whet Appetites

There are certain truths that lie as bait in Scripture. They shout or whisper an invitation to live in a realm and with an experience that will renew our minds, immerse us in God's loving nature and cause us to collide with the cries of the world. Jesus would speak in parables in hopes that the hungry would press in and gain the meaning of what He was trying to teach. In doing so the truth would stay hidden from those who weren't hungry.

Hunger is a fuel that works to burn the veil that keeps us from perceiving things from God's perspective. I have heard it said, "Most of us repent enough to be forgiven, but not enough to see the kingdom." Repentance, meaning to change the way we think, is a movement of the divine upon our minds and spirits and it enables us to see things as they are. Repentance gives us eyes to see and ears to hear. Once we see and hear of His kingdom, a thirst and hunger is consequently implanted within the humble as we are regenerated into a passionate pursuer of God and His realm.

"For He rescued us from the domain of darkness, and transferred us to the kingdom of His beloved Son" (Colossians 1:13). This is one such truth that awakens a hunger within me to know the realm that I've been "transferred" into. This is saying that when we became a believer God took us and established us in His kingdom, which is defined as "royal power, kingship, dominion, rule." This is 100% true. It is the hungry soul who will press into this truth and discover the earth-shattering benefits of living *from* His kingdom.

When we learn to live in His presence and in the kingdom that we've been transferred into, anything can happen. We once received a call to come and minister to a woman who had been incapacitated for months with chronic migraines. She was miserable. We entered her apartment, a few of us surrounded her and I felt that she just needed to have an actual encounter with Jesus. She closed her eyes and I asked her some questions as she located the presence of Jesus. She stood next to Jesus, received His love and the words that He had specifically for her. There was an inner healing and a supernatural peace that fell in the room, and when she opened her eyes from that encounter all her pain was gone. Just a visit into His heavenly presence put an end to her string of pain and illness. Living from the kingdom we've been transferred into gives life, health, wisdom, and a host of His gifts and fruits.

Catching glimpses of what can happen when God's truth and realm are encountered has set me on a mission to live consistently from His voice and His kingdom. The Spirit has been given for the purpose that we may know what He has freely given us (1 Cor. 2:12). His reality and His thoughts have literally been put in us with the intention that we would stretch out and apprehend what He has given to us. It makes good sense that we would affect our world more drastically if we are able to live from His kingdom, where our real life is (Eph. 2:6; Col. 3:3), and put to work all that He has freely given us and made available to us.

Hunger is the desperate brother of curiosity and hunger will cause us to do things as we have become convinced that we cannot live without a thing. In this case, people hungry for His kingdom and righteousness will desperately and joyously press in for what they believe God has already determined to give them.

Hungry and Filled

> "Blessed are those who hunger and thirst for righteousness for they will be filled" (Matthew 5:6).

This whole life has been divinely set up in a manner that will only allow the hungry to be satisfied. Those who are satisfied with their current experience of God will grow bored, religious, predictable, lifeless and will not contribute to the corporate destiny of the redeemed—to bring the realities of heaven to earth. On the other end, those passionately hungry for what is right (God's standard of life, holiness and realities that exist in His kingdom) will be alive with satisfaction as they walk in line with divine purpose.

Being satisfied in God only pleases Him to an extent. If my life does not look like Jesus', with healing, grace, love, power and abundant life swirling about me, then how can I be satisfied with where I am? The hungry and thirsty get filled. They are the only happy and blessed ones who will be satisfied on this earth. Living hungry and thirsty for God and His kingdom is the only means capable of escaping the inevitable boredom that looms, dripping from the tongue of the deceiver. The enemy preaches against the hope of "more", incites satisfaction and stagnation, scheming to perpetuate a people who are anti-hope and anit-expectation, void of faith and content with a salvation that merely escapes eternal demise.

Jesus did not appear on the earth just to save me. This is akin to saying that the purpose of Israel's release from Egypt by the hand of God was simply so they could live free in the desert, dying in the sand. Beyond escape from slavery to sin and fear of death, Jesus came to reveal the real nature of God, give me His very Spirit and empower me to bring the realities of heaven to earth. This is what is possible and we are only limited by our hunger and what we will venture to believe. Our satisfaction depends on it. We were born to transform this world and only the hungry and thirsty will endure, believe, continue in hope and experience the promises.

The Bitter, Sweet and Good

"The satisfied man loathes honey, but to the hungry man any bitter thing is sweet" (Proverbs 27:7). Our contentment and satisfaction, which is usually rooted in pride, will actually lead us to even despise what is sweet. God can give revelation, love, gifts and grace to such people yet their satisfaction will cause them to detest realities that may be flowing directly out of the hand of God. Contentment is an enemy of the spiritual. Dryness that doesn't bother us will act as a guard against our personal revival.

In stark opposition, the man who is hungry for the more of God, who knows that his destiny is God's own righteousness and the likeness of Jesus, will find sweetness, reward, grace and goodness in anything that produces life. The hungry soul is tuned to praise. It is trained in gratitude. It bleeds faith and has a matching expectation for good around every corner. I'm under the conviction that this kind of hunger is only possible when good is anticipated. And good can only be anticipated when we know God's goodness to be only good. A lack of hunger for God and His realm is often rooted in lies that exist in our minds which allow for thoughts that attribute bad things to God's nature, will and activity.

To know God is to long to be near Him. To taste of His goodness will lead to a thirst that words cannot explain. He is good beyond measure and those with this level of faith, expectation and confident hope will be wooed to discover the depths of this alluring love.

Thirsty Years

For years in this Seattle ministry our core group of people would fast together, pray together, worship together and explore the boundaries of the kingdom God says is ours. We would drive across the state, out of the state and fly across the nation to catch a glimpse of something that sounded like the ministry of Jesus. Hunger is inconvenient and costly.

On several occasions, on drives to Spokane, WA, I would stop by the grave of John G. Lake. His life, story and healing ministry are a huge encouragement to me. My thirst for God's kingdom led me to honor people who have carried a tremendous level of His righteousness. I would just sit by his grave and ask God to pour more of Himself out on me, too.

A few years ago, our church was on a fast during Lent where we chose to eat mostly fruits and vegetables. We had felt during this season that the month of May was going to be monumental. We held on and excitedly entered May. During one of our Sunday meetings we had a guest band lead worship for us. They were a young, talented group of musicians from a Seventh-Day Adventist background. Our group enjoys long, lingering worship sets, as we love just hanging out in the Presence. They quickly went through their songs but the Body was desperate for more as the Holy Spirit was really beginning to move. They eventually played another song and then covered a Bob Marley tune as people were dropping like flies (in a good way). It had never really happened before and I don't experience God in this way, but people were losing the ability to stand as His glory filled the dinner theater where we meet. People were laughing and absolutely silly. My mind was helpless to figure this out. Of course, when the Spirit was *first* given the disciples appeared drunk, so I concluded that this was likely a normal response to an outpouring of the Spirit.

The following week during worship there was such a sweet spirit in the room. We hung out for a long time on just a few notes and a few spontaneous lines of worship. Soon we began to hear a multitude singing along with us. Although there were probably just fifty of us in the room, it sounded like a thousand. There was the majestic, hovering sound of a light murmur mixed with a harmony. After the service ended even children's workers in a different room said that is sounded like there were a thousand people singing in there. There had been a heavenly host with us, angels, singing in praise to God with us and we heard them with our physical ears. It probably shouldn't be that hard to believe (see Heb. 12:22).

The string of crazy, awesome worship times continued the following Sunday. I had taught about the joy that is in heaven. Jesus said that one sinner repenting causes heaven to burst into rejoicing (Luke 15:7, 10). Living in a day where multitudes come into the kingdom every day means there is constant, abundant rejoicing there. During the worship that followed the message we were in a total state of celebration before God. Last week the Presence had been sweet and soft. This week the worship was loud and celebratory. As all miracles really are, what occurred is unexplainable. As we rejoiced before God confetti began to fall from the ceiling. We were brought deeper into an awe of God and joy.

During these three weeks of encounters during worship it was clear to us that when our appetite for God and His kingdom is expressed and elevated, especially in atmospheres of worship, then we can expect heaven to respond.

The Hunger-Dependent Gifts

The deep things of God are not available to the casual seeker. It takes all of you going after Him to discover all that is yours in Him.

When God began to stir my heart and show me that miracles, signs and wonders were to be a normal part of my life, I lost sleep. As I mentioned, I would wake, aggravated in my spirit, at 2, 3 or 4 in the morning. I would get up and just spill myself before God. In obedience to the Word I earnestly desired the gifts. I would fast and pray, crying out for an experience of God that would make me dangerous to the present darkness.

The best gifts we could say are ones that are unique to us, they are needed, they are wanted and they are things that will be regularly useful. The gifts God gives meet these criteria and then go deeper. We can know without a doubt that the gifts God would give us will be very useful, they are things/abilities that we need and they will be crafted to mesh with who we are becoming as new creations with divine DNA.

The good Father knows how to give good gifts. And they are gifts that we need in order to fulfill our commission to establish His realities on earth. For example, since there is no sickness in heaven, then I need to operate in the gift of healing in order that my world may look like His. I was not going after healing because I knew someone in need of a healing miracle, but I was hungry for this gift because God had made it available to me. Jesus obviously walked with this gift, and I had been instructed to "earnestly desire" it. And it was only as I sought after this gift, and others, that fruit began to follow.

The first of His gifts began to manifest for me after two years of pressing in. Abbi experienced gifts coming out of her nearly by accident, but for me it took two years of pursuit. I believe that a large part of my barrier to the supernatural was my logical mind. Perhaps one of the most frustrating revelations to the spiritually educated is that God is pleased to hide kingdom authority from and wise and intelligent (Luke 10:21). God reveals His deep things like power and authority over diseases and demons to children—hungry, naïve, joyful, believing, un-offendable children.

Go Get Gifts!

Putting spiritual gifts in a Christmas context, if these gifts from the God of all creation sat underneath a Christmas tree, I should be so beside myself in curious awe, wondering what kind of perfect gift lay there. The nine gifts He makes available to us are ones that will build us into the likeness of Christ, transform our minds and enable us to be a walking testament of who God is (2 Cor. 3:3). Let it be emphasized that these gifts are available and not necessarily an automatic. Expectant faith and movement are required of us to go and unwrap these gifts that all have our names on them.

The gifts sit labeled "under the tree" yet I have tended to misunderstand the word "gift". In regard to these gifts, I used to acknowledge them and then make the choice of whether or not I wanted one of them based on my understanding of it. Another unproductive approach is assuming that if God wants me to have the gifts then He will give them to me. This forsakes one of the first elements of the Christian faith, which is that He has already given them to us. "Freely you have received, freely give" is said in the context of Jesus giving kingdom authority to the disciples and sending them out to heal the sick, raise the dead and proclaim the nearness of God's kingdom realities (Mt 10:8). The gifts lie within the realm of the Spirit and we have been given the Holy Spirit and "every spiritual blessing in the heavenly places in Christ" (Eph. 1:3). They lie within us in seed form. Our hunger, faith and pursuit in prayer over these things that God already has chosen to give us act like water on these seeds.

"Desire earnestly the spiritual gifts" (1 Cor. 14:1). We are to earnestly and passionately, jealously and lustfully (as the Greek implies) desire the spiritual gifts. We are to passionately want to heal, perform miracles, have supernatural wisdom, faith, knowledge, etc. These gifts have our names on them and the One who gives them is not offended by our pursuit of them. An excited recipient is a huge blessing to the giver. Imagine a child looking upon a gift and remarking, "It seems dangerous." "I don't know..." "Well, if you really want me to have it you'll have to open it for me and give it to me." I feel that God may respond as we would if our child reacted in this manner: "It is an amazing gift. But if you want to experience it you're going to have to go discover it."

Activation Required

Though God's spiritual (supernatural) gifts may be in us for free, the development of these gifts requires our involvement, desire and an all-in faith. Paul addressed Timothy *reminding* him (which implies Paul had already instructed Timothy on this matter) to stir up, or kindle afresh, the gift that was in him (2 Tim. 1:6). *You. You* go stir it up and activate it, putting it to use. This is possible, Timothy, because God has not given you a spirit that would make you shy, but He has put within you a spirit of power, one full of love, and He has conveniently given you a spirit of discipline and sound thinking so that you will be able to make yourself do the supernatural works that you're destined for (2 Tim. 1:7). These gifts require activation. They require that we tend to them and stir them up and into action.

When do we get to conclude that we do not have the gift of healing? After we pray for our dying mother and she still dies? After we "fail" ten times? Asking these questions is of itself evidence of unbelief. I started to pray for the sick out in public not because I wanted to see if I had the gift of healing but because Jesus sent me, as a Christian, to do so. He did not send me empty-handed. He equipped me with power, love and discipline. He gave me authority over every sickness and disease and evil spirit, bar none. Yet this gift had to be pursued earnestly (1 Cor. 14:1) as I went and prayed for the sick. We do not merely pursue the gift by asking for it to become more evident. We cry out for the healing anointing to become manifest and we look for and expect it to become manifest as we set out in loving obedience to meet people in their pain.

Stir it Up

Convinced that God always wants to move and use me to release heaven's power to those around me in need, I feel like I am in a dry season when I have not seen any recent miracles. I don't want to bore my angels or allow the fire of the Spirit or the gifts within me to grow dim or dull. Whenever I enter seasons that are dry I usually just make a trip to the Emergency Room. An advantage we have by living in central Seattle is that there are five major hospitals I can be at in minutes. When I feel that the supernatural power of God in me has not been activated in awhile then I am compelled to find someone who needs a miracle.

Whether or not a miracle actually takes place, my spirit and joy are stirred when I reach in and attempt to use God's gifts. Life is awakened within me when hunger drives me to obediently move into someone else's need for a God encounter. Even when I step out in sheer discipline, rather than passion, faith or hunger, my spirit is injected with life and joy.

I distinctly remember going into an ER and sitting down next to the first person I saw that looked in pain. She was holding her stomach and having trouble breathing. She just sat there with her eyes closed, trying to cope with the pain. I introduced myself and asked how she was doing. She told me about her stomach pain, the pregnancy and several other issues she was dealing with that landed her here in this hospital. She agreed to let me pray for her and we just invited the Holy Spirit to come as we released His presence and healing onto her body. In the middle of that crowded ER there was a cool breeze that gently came over us. There were no windows or doors open, and no vents blowing, yet I could physically feel a calm breeze. The Holy Spirit was moving in the room and the pain in her stomach lessened and her migraine and feverish temperature was relieved immediately.

I have come to understand that our hunger is in our hands. I am able to stir up hunger in my spirit if I find myself bored. Getting connected in amazement with God is key. A fruit of the hungry life is that we will live in awe and praise of God. I knew I was intended to live releasing power like Jesus and as I pursued that kind of lifestyle a tremendous amount of awe and wonder accompanied that hunger.

Religion tends to guard and create boundaries, limits and rules. It will seek to bring explanation to everything so that everything can be neat and tidy. But hunger aggravates our spirits and moves us out of places of comfort and into situations where we are vulnerable and in desperate need of God to show up.

Process and Training

Americans want things immediately and without effort. In our recent history we have become marked as a people who don't wait well as we long for our fulfilled desires. The value of process is a revelation that had long eluded me. The Hebrews passage that we've already looked at is a gem of wisdom that helped me in my search for the more of God. The "more" in this verse is referred to as "solid food", as opposed to the milk that the people had not graduated from due to their inability to hear well in their spirit.

"But solid food is for the mature, who because of practice have their senses trained to discern good and evil" (Hebrews 5:14).

Firstly, notice that the deep things of God are reserved for the mature. This is describing the one who is perfect and lacking nothing. These people have agreed to a process of purification and training whereby they constantly and continuously, as a lifestyle, lived in such an obedient way to the instructions of Jesus that they were then able to know what was good and evil. I wouldn't have thought that I needed to be moving purposefully toward maturity in order to know what was God's activity and what was the enemy's. But to those who have "trained their senses", exercised their perception through practice, divine understanding is reached. It may sound too lofty but this is the meaning of "maturity" here.

What I really want to stress from the verse is the single New Testament use of this word "practice" (ἕξις). It is defined as a habit, and "a power acquired by custom, practice, use."[9] It is because of habitual use that we walk into a mature healing gift or any other gift. (A mature healing gift would be marked by its frequent effectiveness in bringing health and life.) Maturity, holiness and anointing don't just happen. People don't just wake up and decide to establish the kingdom of God in fullness today. No, it is through faith and perseverance that we inherit what is promised (Hebrews 6:12). And hunger that is tethered to biblical faith will provide the perspective necessary to endure until the promise of the Word becomes our experienced reality. Our gifts, like our "senses", are trained through constant use and practice.

Hunger's Reward

Once I began to enjoy the process and move out in risk, joy and obedience to Matthew 10:8, I found that faith was being multiplied

---

[9] http://www.blueletterbible.org/lang/lexicon/lexicon.cfm?Strongs=G1838&t=NASB

in me. I became more aware of God's presence, I felt His power in me, and I was feeling more and more bold and experiencing a manifold joy. I was enjoying these benefits even while people were rarely even getting healed when I prayed for them, because moving in supernatural power is not the goal of the Christian life. My perfection is tied to being the beloved, enjoying the full benefits of the new creation that Jesus purchased for me as I obediently follow His commands and enjoy His presence. As I, full of faith and expectation, attempt to live as Jesus did and pursue my destiny of Christlikeness (literally) and declare "the kingdom of heaven is near", I am fulfilling my call as a follower of Jesus. There is no such thing as failure. The only categories for how this spiritual life is lived seem to be either faith or fear and unbelief. Hunger pulls on heaven, stretches for the hem of His robe, pants for His righteousness to be see in me and knocks over the Christmas tree in bursting joy over what these gifts could possible do for my city.

The promise of reward hangs over those who drop everything else to engage on the pursuit of a lifetime. "He who comes to God must believe that He is and that He is a rewarder of those who seek Him" (Heb. 11:6). Pursuit comes with reward.

Setting Out

Hunger moves people. Appetite for God and His kingdom puts you into motion. Flowing from the throne of His love, His kingdom and His gifts are so compelling that they stir us into action even when we have no idea what we are doing, what we are saying or where we are going.

Back to Safeway. I made this trek several times a week when I lived near this particular store as I had either small children or a pregnant wife who was craving something specific. I knew that I was likely to encounter someone who was either in pain or needed "a dose of the Ghost". It's inconvenient to live listening to the Holy Spirit if our main goal day in and day out is to get things done quickly and efficiently. Each time at the store in my season of training my senses through habitually releasing the good news of a happy God, I knew that I would come across someone who was depressed, broken, in pain or someone who even made eye contact with me.

Living on His frequency was exhilarating. I was learning that He's always talking, giving me impressions, words or always wanting to do something. I didn't use to live knowing that. I may have verbally lined up with this truth but I sure didn't experientially live in the truth that He is very likely going to speak to me, through me and use me to make manifest His kingdom each and every day. Life became a thrill beyond measure when I chose to embed this truth into my every cell. And many of my cells didn't like it. Especially the ones who loved to live in the natural, in comfort, in logic, in safe places behind walls where there would be no humiliation. Yet the worst humiliations are elevators to the Throne Room.

My hunger for the things of God led me to experiment with what He said was true of me. Since He said I had power to heal diseases I wanted to experiment (experience) with this truth. The hunger for His kingdom and for His righteousness to be revealed through me drove me to face my fear of rejection. Desperate hunger will do foolish things like that. Fears stand no chance against real hunger. Yet our hunger will move us into places that will cause us to have to deal with fear. When I first started understanding that God wanted to heal people in public places through my obedience I was so perplexed and filled with concern and anxiety. But my hunger for His kingdom come was so great that it caused me to deal with my desire for approval and how I had lived to avoid conflict. Being a people with an assignment to bring heaven to earth and destroy the works of the devil, we are invited into conflict. Our conflict is not with people but with the doings of the enemy (who causes pain, sickness, bondage, poverty, etc.). Engaging in this conflict is part of what it means to be salt and light. We are to step in where there is lack and bring transformation.

> "To walk with God in the high places we must lose our fear. Fear can only be lost in the desert, in the crucible of warfare, inferiority and internal struggle. In the place where only God can shelter you."[10]

The Rarity of Aged Desperation

My Grandpa Rodes demonstrated a hungry and humble heart better than anyone I know. After decades in the ministry he had an authentic fire and desperation for God. He cried out to Him every morning, soaked in the Word and then would joyfully recite

[10] Graham Cooke, "The Journey of Discovering the Depths of God's Love for You," *Living in Dependency and Wonder* (England: Sovereign World, 2004), p. 5.

His favorite verses to me in fresh amazement. I remember staying with Him while we were moving to start seminary. I was in wonder of his zeal that surpassed my own. He was "retiring" from ministry (which he never successfully did) and I was about to begin. It was my hope then that I would continue to grow in awe of God until my last days just as he did.

The Sunday before he passed to make the physical transfer into the fullness of God's kingdom, he was said to be dancing in worship to the God he never stopped responding to. His childlike faith and hunger and his desire to learn from even his grandchildren cemented him as a model for those who wish to be poor in spirit and hunger for righteousness. Growing old and yet simultaneously enjoying hunger pangs and yearnings was a miraculous quality of his life, and it has yielded a lineage of those who have now given themselves to full-time ministry. Because Grandpa served God and people with irrepressible joy, freedom and hunger for the things of God, those who watched his life were compelled to follow.

Royal Hunger

Hunger demonstrates humility. Our hunger demonstrates that we are living with some lack. We long for something that we do not yet have. And we want it desperately. It is a bit challenging to understand completely, but part of the goodness and glory of God is revealed in that He conceals things for us, and the glory within humanity compels them to search and find what God is holding for us. "It is the glory of God to conceal a matter, but the glory of kings is to search out a matter" (Proverbs 25:2). Hunger creates royal character within us, and it works as a refining fire in us. It prepares the wineskin of our spirit to be able to receive and walk in what God has intended for us.

God entrusts the destinies of cities to the hungry. Psalm 107:36 reveals a fascinating aspect of the mind of God. He intends to build healthy cities by putting hungry people at the foundation of this process. "And there He makes the hungry to dwell, so that they may establish an inhabited city." Divine favor rests on those who live aware of their need for God and have also committed themselves to have that appetite met. Most believers have no problem identifying their need for God. Yet those who will hunger and thirst after righteousness and His kingdom, pressing in to obtain the gifts and realities that He says are ours are a rare breed that exemplify a faith and perseverance that bend the heavens with joy.

The kingdom of heaven belongs to the hungry and the humble inherit the earth. When the humble are hungry for more of God's kingdom, they are the ones that can be trusted. They are the ones who will answer the prayer "Your will be done, on earth as it is in heaven." They will walk in kingdom power and authority and see their world begin to look like His. Kingdom authority is hidden from the wise but revealed to those who are like children—hungry, humble and full of faith.

Hunger and humility draw a response from heaven, as they are united with faith. And it is to the issue of faith that we now turn. Hunger and humility may position us to draw from heavenly resources, but it is faith that enables any transaction to actually occur.

7

FAITH INHERITS PROMISES

Faith is simply and obviously presented as one of the most powerful dimensions of the spiritual life. It literally opens up doors of the impossible and can usher in the will and kingdom of God.

Believe More Than You Doubt

Believe more than you doubt. It is now shocking to me that this was a revelation. But it was something that Holy Spirit needed to soak into my soul. This demonstrated how far I had "advanced" out of biblical faith. It seemed that the more I had learned with my mind the more I was moved into a barren, intellectual desert, where I was able to explain more yet experienced less of what a Christ-filled life should look like under a New Covenant where the very Spirit of God is living inside each believer. The more

I "understood", the more predictable, human and awe-less this anointed-ian (Christian) life became.

Faith, on the other hand, opens us up to mysteries, the impossible and the realm of the Spirit where we are not confined by what we can understand or control. We are to be believers. People who believe. We believe in Jesus, His life, death and resurrection. We believe in a new creation—people born anew from above and restored to the image of God. But I realized that when it came to really believing that God has intended to powerfully work through His creation, co-laboring with us to restore a broken earth, fractured hearts and diseased bodies, I tended to bend toward uncertainty, skepticism, unbelief, and doubt. While undergoing the battle for true faith it seemed that I was okay with believing anything that still left me without responsibility. Was my light supposed to bring transformation to the world or was I supposed to just pray that God would do His thing? It was likely in my subconscious, but my flesh and intellect would rise to remain in control and keep me from real faith—the kind that terrifies the devil and ushers in God's kingdom and His will.

Absurd, Naïve Faith

In seminary, a fellow student accused my dad of being biblically naïve. The hovering implication being, you can't really take the Word at face value.

"Ask and it will be given to you" (Matthew 7:7).

This is one of the many promises of Jesus that can cause difficulty. The problem is that we have tried this "asking" and experienced it *not* being given to us. But a faith that pleases God is one that continues to hope even when our experience of the promise has still eluded us. Faith in the powerful claims of Jesus regarding our authority and influence makes many nervous because there is a fear of causing false hope. One thing that my heart was set on was not allowing my disappointments to lower the level of my belief in the Word or expectation of the fulfillment of His promises. I want absurd, naïve faith, for I have the burning sense that it will take such confidence in His word to accomplish the impossible things that He's wooed me into dreaming. It will take such *believers* to experience the biblical truths that are available to us. But take note: these experiences are not available to all. They are available to all who *believe* —expecting and anticipating.

The Choice

When making the journey from religion to faith, I found that I was continuously faced with opportunities to attribute an occurrence to the activity of God or to coincidence or my own imagination. Several years ago, as our church was in prayer asking God for His heart for us in this season, He helped us "craft" a prayer (See the book, Crafted Prayer[11]) that we could pray out regularly knowing we

11 Graham Cooke, "The Joy of Always Getting Your Prayers Answered," *Crafted Prayer* (England: Sovereign World, 2003).

were praying in line with the heart of God for us. It went like this:

> God, raise up a unified people, who, in authority, care about the poor, care about the broken, care about transformation and seeking first your kingdom and righteousness.

God even gave our Body a powerful song that was based on this prayer. Months later we had an intern come to live with us. In His first week He got a letter from one of his prayer supporters and she gave him some encouragement. In the middle of this letter, she wrote out our "crafted prayer" word for word. As our intern, Seth, showed us the letter he said, "Don't you guys have a song with some of those words?" Looking at the letter I was shocked, seeing that the prayer she had written was our exact prayer.

The mind and spirit that live in caution immediately think, as I did then, "Is this prayer on our website? She must've seen this prayer on our website." We often storm through all the scenarios that are likely and logical and if the event survives the challenge and interrogation of logic, then we'll succumb and be amazed with God and perhaps even acknowledge that we've experienced something miraculous and been involved in something where God's fingerprint landed.

I realized that we likely experience so little of His activity because we don't start from a place of faith. We often start in doubt and work backwards toward faith. For a spiritual person my first response should be, "Look what God has done!" If I went on to learn later that the prayer partner had a copy of our prayer somehow, would my faith be destroyed? No. Who cares? "Oh, so you got it from the website. We were amazed, thinking that God used your hand to write our church's heart on that letter." God probably won't get mad if we accidentally, through belief in His activity and goodness, give Him credit for something He didn't do. The truth is, there no danger in assuming God has been actively good in a situation.

I'm becoming more and more impressed that I need to assume God's been active, that He's moving among us. This must be my starting place. As it's becoming my starting place I'm finding that I'm experiencing more verified miracles. It seems as though I've had to show myself to be a believer first—one who believes first, without a jury and not as a lawyer putting supposed miracles on trial. I'm attempting to live simply. Live believingly. After all, "love believes all things" (1 Cor. 13:7). I don't need to see a doctors' report to verify a healing. I choose to believe.

Following Jesus' most awkward teaching, the demand that His very flesh and blood be chewed and drank, many of His disciples turned away from Him. Turning to the twelve He asked, "You do not want to go away also, do you?" Peter speaks up and points out, "Lord, to whom shall we go? You have words of eternal life. We have believed and have come to know that You are the Holy One of God" (John 6:67-69). They believed and then they came to know what they had already believed. The work "know" (γινώσκω), here, refers to an intimate knowledge. It is a New Testament word used to describe an intimate, experiential knowledge. Knowing is experiencing. As we believe we will also come to know and gain an intimate experience.

We should believe for more than we are experiencing. The Bible is limitless in what we have permission to believe for. Whatever we've read of others experiencing in God through the Bible, we can legally say, "That's possible for me"—the sun standing still, seas dividing, dead raising, ax heads floating, the barren giving birth, revival hitting a town because one man released the kingdom of God. We must believe for more than we are experiencing. And biblical belief means that we are expecting and anticipating what we are believing for. To not expect to experience what I am believing for is called doubt, not faith, because faith has expectancy. And faith is not judged or modified by negative experiences.

What About Mom?

While strolling my young son through the grocery store one day we came upon a young woman working in an aisle. I gave a general greeting and asked how she was doing as we passed by. Most people say, "Fine", even if they're not. But she actually gave an honest response: "Oh, my back hurts." I stopped the shopping cart and doubled back to follow up with the employee. She explained how she had tweaked her back and that she was in a lot of pain. Sam and I released healing and she looked up at us, smiled and found the pain to be gone!

I leaned over to Sam as I pushed him in the shopping cart and explained to him that God just healed that girl's back. "Isn't that amazing?!" His reply was sobering. "But momma's still sick, right?"

Yes, Abbi's migraines remain and while I don't understand why others get healed and she hasn't yet, I cannot allow the mystery of what *hasn't* happened choke my praise or cloud my expectation of God's desire to move today. Holding God hostage with our questions only reveals unbelief. While living in mystery can be very painful, I am learning to just trust His goodness and I will never say that it must be His will for some evil (pain) to persist. Jesus has already clearly revealed His will concerning pain.

Mystery and Belief

I have prayed for years, with my community, for the healing of one of our dear friend's children who suffers horrible seizures. Her condition halted her development at 6 months of age. Nine years has past with little change. We are all regularly confronted with the option to stop believing that we have authority over all sickness and disease (Luke 9:1). Our experience does not nullify the words of Jesus. We can make sound arguments and allow our natural reality to "mature" us out of childlike faith. We have that option. Or we can continue to believe that what Jesus has said of us is still true, truer than what we perceive with our natural senses, and thus give the Word opportunity to become our experienced ("known") reality. We will come to know (experience) *as we have believed.*

My desire is to be so swallowed in God, so aware of His smile and whisper, given over to the subtle thoughts that He floats across my heart and mind that I live with fearless love, always erring on the side of faith. To be sure, I would rather be on trial for having too much faith rather than for living from a mode that defaults to doubt. Even if I'm wrong and I've acted out of faith, being sure of what you hope for and confident of what you cannot see (Hebrews 11:1), I believe that the pleasure of God is over me. He loves it when people believe and move out in expectation on what they believe. On the other hand, those who are incredibly calculated and never fail, yet rarely move out in faith (which John Wimber has said is spelled R-I-S-K), I can't help but imagine that the Spirit of God is grieved. "Without faith it is impossible to please Him" (Hebrews 11:6). God longs for us to experience our fullness and significance which faith makes available.

When Jesus returns He is not going to be primarily concerned with whether or not we've been careful, performed miracles or had perfect attendance in church. He'll be concerned about whether or not He will find faith on the earth (Luke 18:8).

Testing the Principle

A few years into my Seattle ministry I discovered that God wanted to bring me into an experience of everything I believed. Until a truth is experienced it seems to be more of a theory or principle. In 2004 God invited us into a season of experiencing Him as provider and testing the principle of sowing and reaping. Believing that God would always give to us more than we could give away (Luke 6:38; Malachi 3:10; 2 Cor. 9:6), we felt compelled to give money and stuff away in order to get debt free. Our student loans exceeded 33,000. By our choice, we decided to put everything in our apartment up for sale. This was so excruciating for Abbi that she could not be present during the estate sale. Nearly half of everything went out the door that day and we gave many pieces of furniture away as well as a good amount of cash.

With everything we gave away, much more money would miraculously come in. With whatever God poured back into our laps we would give away half of it (sowing it) and the other half we would put toward our debt. Within a year and a half our debt shrank from 33,000 to 3,000. Not only were we nearly out of debt, but our home had better stuff than before. The new stuff that came from God was actually closer to our style. I remember looking around the living room and seeing the awesome chairs, a vintage couch and so many others things that had just been *given* to us. It seemed risky and made little sense, but faith will put to test the things we hold to be true. Faith is not satisfied with a belief that has not been experienced.

Reckless Faith

Because of my increasing distaste for doubt, the antichrist of the supernatural life, one of my many favorite words I have read outside the Bible was from Smith Wigglesworth.

> "God rocked in a man makes a man rocked in God and so submitted to God that there is no carefulness."[12]

---

[12] Roberts Liardon, "On Prayer, Power and Miracles," *Smith Wigglesworth* (Shippensburg, PA: Destiny Image Publishers, 2006), p. 13.

It is possible for the activity and promptings of the Spirit to be so alive within us that it will trample any trepidation. Jesus, who lived completely aware of the thoughts and will of God, doing and saying what He was doing and saying, never stalled wondering if what He was about to do would offend others, humiliate Himself or bring Him rejection. He lived to bring life and His kingdom.

Faith is bold. The word "careful" is only used once in the New Testament. Once! (We'll talk about the other word translated "careful" in a moment.) The one appearance of "careful" is used to instruct us to "speak confidently, so that those who have believed God will be careful to engage in good deeds. These things are good and profitable for men" (Titus 3:8). Be careful to engage in good deeds. Even the word "careful" in this passage finds its derivative in the word φϱήν, "understanding." Our carefulness is measured by our understanding and ability to see. If God is asking us to be careful it will only be in the context of Him urging us to see accurately, from His perspective, and move with His understanding.

The majority of the Old Testament passages on being "careful" have to do with obeying what God has instructed us and assigned us to. Carrying this over in the New Testament, our carefulness and attentiveness to His commands has as much to do with healing the sick and casting out demons as it does with loving others and turning our cheek when wronged. We have been given a few, precise orders of conduct, and healing the sick is not optional. It's what we do as Christians. Be careful to obey. Don't let this one slip out of your sight, mind or awareness. It is important to know what He is asking of us so that we know what we are to be faithful to.

There's a passage in Ephesians 5:15 which explains that our careful (the Greek word here literally means "to see accurately") living has to do with making the most of every opportunity and destroying evil. It is living careful, so that we're not ineffective or doing nothing while evil is busy. The picture of sowing seed in Matthew 13 does not depict a careful sower but a reckless one, scattering seed everywhere! This is an image of our lives in the kingdom.

We've exalted the "virtue" of carefulness over fire, zeal and boldness. We've become tactful and polished, safe and ineffective. Paul and Peter, two of the men that God chose to establish our faith on the earth were chosen, I believe, because of their personalities. Peter was never known for being cautious and God, in His wisdom, chose to build the church on him (Matthew 16:18). God has not given us a spirit of timidity. The root of this word used in 2 Timothy 1:7 is "fearfulness". It has been my experience that much of my carefulness and hesitancy to demonstrate His kingdom was really rooted in my own fears. God has, however, given us a spirit of power, love and a sound mind/ discipline (2 Timothy 1:7). We're given a spirit of discipline and a sound mind along with power and love so that we are able to make ourselves do and think what we are supposed to do and think, in line with the heart and mind of God, in all boldness and certainty. The only people that entered the Promised Land from the desert were Joshua and Caleb because they were the only ones who believed God and didn't succumb to a fear that was based on obstacles in the natural. Fear is faithlessness, caution is doubt, and true wisdom gives divine tactics that will catapult us into moves of love and power.

Our Caution is "Seeing"

Other verses in the New Testament that give the translation "beware" or "take heed" come from the Greek word that simply means "to see, or discern." Thus, Christian carefulness is really just living in reality, truth and seeing things and situations as they are. If we're cautious about anything, it has to do with being obedient to what God has already clearly laid out for us to do. If we don't know what to do, we fall back on what He has already told us to do—love people, forgive, heal the sick, etc. These are the constants. The immutable. They don't ever alter.

Faith is active and because it lives with expectation it will drive people into an activity that longs to see the fruit of what they hold in their hearts. Faith lives with a green light because it is convinced that God is happy, is love and is always wanting to invade our world with power, love and life. I have heard it said, "All it takes for evil to succeed is for good people to do nothing." People who jump on every opportunity to bless others are writing the brand of Christianity that is changing the world and they live to create opportunities for God to move. If we wait for optimal conditions to do good, we will rarely do good.

The "virtue of carefulness" will also lead believers to value doubt as a form of wisdom. If I am skeptical of miracles because I haven't seen any then I am required to change the way I think and align my mind with the Christian gospel that clearly says that miracles are the norm. To take it a step further, suppose I want to believe that healings and miracles are for today but I just want to verify their authenticity. The western mind complies with this mindset but this, too, is not entirely biblical. Jesus did not respond well to attitudes that demanded proofs and signs. "An adulterous generation asks for a sign" (Mt. 12:39; Mt. 16:4). Not believing what God has said over our experience is likened to marital unfaithfulness. We're cheating on God and becoming nestled up next to doubt. We may call it wisdom, carefulness, prudence or a host of other names. But the fact remains, "These signs will follow those who believe: in My name they will cast out demons... they will lay hands on the sick, and they will recover" (Mark 16:17-18). The word "follow" is stating here that miraculous signs will always accompany so "as to always be at his side". The Word is true and our lives and theology must be transformed so that we become who God has said we already are.

Love Believes

Being in love with God will not lead to questioning everything until it proves true. We are to believe and *then* experience. When I first began to ask God about the issue of authority and whether or not it was really true for me, all I heard Him say was "I give you authority." And when I started to see miracles (or very amazing coincidences) I didn't want to be lead astray so I would ask God, "Were you really behind that one?" "Was that true?" And He would reply, "Do you want it to be true?" As I see it now, God was inviting me into faith. I began to realize that He was not really concerned about whether or not I gave Him too much credit. He's not worried about us believing too much as we endeavor to live life like Jesus. Then came this revelation: "Love believes all things" (1 Cor. 13:7). Faith is the fruit of being in love.

We learn from the first followers of Jesus that our thinking and believing must be able to be molded by the experience of other believers whom we know. Their experience of God and His power is not only to elevate them but those who hear of it as well.

After Jesus rose from the dead, as it is recorded in the gospel of Mark, it is said that He appeared to Mary Magdalene and then again to two others. All three told the disciples they had seen Jesus but they refused to believe. When Jesus appeared to the eleven disciples the first thing He did was reproach them for their unbelief. Sounds harsh. But Jesus is getting ready to leave these guys in charge of bringing the gospel of the kingdom and revival (these terms are synonymous) to the world and He makes it known how serious of an issue unbelief is. "He reproached them for their unbelief and hardness of heart, because they had not believed those who had seen Him after He had risen" (Mark 16:9-15). The I'll-believe-it-when-I-see-it mentality is antithetical to the gospel. Doubt and skepticism is the complete opposite spirit of faith and it is something that must be overcome, not embraced as a virtue. Belief makes you a candidate to experience that which you "are sure you are hoping for" (Heb. 11:1), while unbelief, doubt and skepticism actually work to insulate and protect you from the promises and power of His Word.

Belief will beget conflict because we are attempting to live by faith over sight. Often, His kingdom invades ours to the degree that we are able to agree with what He has said over what we can naturally perceive. Faith pulls His kingdom into ours.

The Faith Hinge

Whenever people are not being healed, I never accuse them of not having enough faith. This sort of judgment runs contrary to a spirit of love and service. The pain and damage that is caused by pointing fingers may be worse than the diseases we are hoping to defeat. There have been many abuses that have taken place through such judgments, yet my heart races with some key faith instructions from Jesus.

Jesus was questioned about whether or not He could deliver a man's son who was unable to speak because of a demon. The demon would throw the son to the ground and the even the disciples could not bring deliverance and healing. The father said to Jesus, "'If you can do anything, take pity on us and help us.' And Jesus said to him, 'If You can?' All things are possible to him who believes'" (Mark 9:22-23).

The responsibility for the healing was put on Jesus, but Jesus turned the tables and said the deliverance had more to do with one's ability to believe. The problem is *never* whether or not God is able or if a healing is His will. The issue lies with us. Are we able to believe?

The gravity of the centrality of faith is not intended to cause condemnation, guilt or shame. We must avoid the urge to explain or solve the mystery of what *didn't* happen. Yet we must simultaneously acknowledge that faith is simply and obviously presented as one of the most powerful dimensions of the spiritual life. It literally opens up doors of the impossible and can usher in the will and kingdom of God. The father of the son was wondering if there was any hope. But the problem was not in the will or power of God. God wanted to heal him. The solution was the present ability to believe. Remember, it was unbelief that restricted Jesus from performing many miracles in His hometown (Mt. 13:58).

On another occasion Jesus addressed two blind men with the simple question, "Do you believe that I am able to do this?" They said, "Yes, Lord." "Then He touched their eyes, saying, 'It shall be done to you according to your faith'" (Mt. 9:28-29). It will happen for you as you are able to believe. In both the Mark 9 and the Matthew 9 passage, the miracle hinged upon the presence and power of faith.

Faith in itself is a power that pulls on heaven and from the virtue of Jesus. We also see this truth with the woman with the issue of blood. Her faith and expectation took hold of a healing without Jesus even releasing the healing. Jesus says, "Who touched me?" "I felt power leave. Who did that?" Her faith, that if she just touched His robe she would be healed, activated the healing. And it was done for her as she believed (Luke 8:43-48; Mark 5:25-34; Mt. 9:20-26). It seems that her story became widespread as later in Mark's gospel we see that *everyone* who touched the fringe of Jesus' cloak were being cured (Mark 6:56). They found out, "Hey, all you have to do is touch His clothes and you get healed. You don't have to wait for Him to pray for you! Just touch Him." Those who moved out with faith and this expectation got exactly what they had expected.

Faith Inherits Promises

Belief opens the door for truth to become our experienced reality. This is the message behind Hebrew 4:2, which gives insight into why the nation of Israel did not experience the promises of God. "For indeed we have had good news preached to us, just as they also; but the word they heard did not profit them, because it was not united by faith in those who heard it" (Hebrews 4:2). God has so conditioned the world and made His will and promises so dependent upon our will and faith that it is said that if we will not believe and agree and accept what the Word has said then the promises (His word) will not profit us. What God said of us (we have authority, power, etc.) must meet our faith and full acceptance in order for that Word to become our reality.

This belief is the deepest message behind the life of Abraham, our Old Testament model, who believed God when He had no proof, and that belief-before-seeing was said to be his righteousness. Meaning, this is the right way to live in relationship with God and His truths. You believe what He said is true not because it's been your experience but because the words came from His mouth or the life of Jesus, His Living Word.

"[Be] imitators of those who through faith and patience inherit the promises" (Hebrews 6:12). Abraham experienced the promises of God and a supernatural life because He had a ridiculous faith and a violent endurance. When all his circumstances defied what was promised, he believed anyway. And it was this faith and endurance that enabled and qualified Abraham to obtain the promise (Romans 4:18). Intimately connected with faith is the issue of endurance, to which we now turn.

8

ENDURANCE AND JOY

When our faith (what we hope for, believe to be true and are certain of in our spirits) comes under fire and is tested, we know good is right around the corner.

Did I Get it Wrong?

In 2011 we bought a house in the Central District of Seattle. We felt peace about it and God seemed to pave the way as we relocated our family twelve blocks from our previous residence. Inside the first month I woke up one morning to see yellow tape by the street outside my son's window. A man had been beat to death on our street. Over that first year there were several murders, innocent people killed in crossfire, burglaries, police raids, constant drug deals, screaming, cussing, and fighting all within two blocks of our home. Positioned on the corner of a noisy street that is cluttered with shouts, the bass from car stereos is constantly vibrating my single-pane windows. The chaos was wearing my peace thin. Though we naturally wondered if we made a good decision, it produced nothing positive in us when we wandered into regret or doubt.

Whenever endurance is needed it seems that the accompanying questions are: "Did I miss something?" Did I get it wrong?" These questions, founded in doubt or uncertainty, stem from the false conclusion that if God is in a thing then there will be no resistance. While checking to see if we heard Him right is permissible, *living* with uncertainty will be toxic to our destiny, which requires perseverance. Questioning my direction and the promises of God when things get hard doesn't usually produce spiritual fruit.

Immediately after God voiced that He was pleased with Jesus, "Jesus was led up by the Spirit into the wilderness" (Matthew 3:17-4:1). God makes our paths straight (Pr. 3:6) but this does not mean that our paths will be without testing and conflict. Again, it is testing and perseverance that give rise to holiness and perfection (James 1:2-4). As with Jesus, it is often the pleasure and favor of God over us that brings us into situations where our faith will be tested. The fastest way into maturity in the Spirit is through crucibles, and through pressures that squeeze our faith and hope. Enduring faith and relentless joy are evidences of maturity. In such circumstances, it is our joy that demonstrates that we know God is not mad, He's not responsible for evil things happening and we sleep well at night knowing that He's pleased with us.

Faith and Patience Change the World

Joined to the requirement of faith is the need of endurance. Faith implies that there is something that we do not yet see or understand yet we choose to trust. Living in faith is living in tension. And living in tension requires a persevering spirit that holds steadily onto the good nature of God and His promises. A person of endurance refuses to lower the high standard of Jesus or change direction even when what we experience seems to contradict the clear message of His Word over our lives.

Without faith and endurance none of us have the hope of enjoying the lofty destiny God has in store for us. Rich promises and victories over the impossible lie ahead of each believing believer. And we are to be "imitators of those who through faith and patience (endurance) inherit the promises" (Hebrews 6:12). What we will be called to pursue as Christians calling God's kingdom into the natural realm will bring conflict and opposition. And it is the enduring soul living by every word that is coming out of the mouth of God who will enjoy the promises.

Perseverance

"Let perseverance finish its work, that you may become mature and complete, lacking nothing" (James 1:4).

In order to be trusted with the deep things of God and the resources of heaven we must demonstrate ourselves to be mature. We are able to praise God in the midst of trial. We're not prone to complaining. We know how to suffer well—with joy. We are able, in complete sincerity to count it a joy when we face trials of many kinds (James 1:2) because we know what they produce. We know what trails do to us and in us. The nature of God and how He works are not optional revelations for those who desire to be used to shape the course of history.

When our faith (what we hope for, believe to be true and are certain of in our spirits) comes under fire and is tested, we know good is right around the corner. It would be grand if we could mature and grow in God apart from trial, but that's not the way things have been set up in the spiritual life. Our growth occurs when we lean into the problems that confront our beliefs and we endure, holding on to the Word and the promises that He's given us, not ever calling His goodness into question, but remaining steadfast and in His peace and joy. We call His goodness into question whenever we attribute bad things to God. Saying that God gave someone sickness, "took" a loved one, or sent a hurricane to punish a city is to take the clear revelation of the nature of God in the person of Jesus and lay it aside.

Perspective changes everything. When we know that our current trials are producing endurance and patience and leading us into a place where we are complete and lacking nothing, what is there to complain about? We can sincerely find joy in it for we are feeling the pleasure of God over us as He forms His nature in us, which lacks nothing. He has no plan for us that is anywhere short of us manifesting His very nature. The fastest, surest way to get us shaped into Jesus' nature is to embrace difficulty and squeeze all the joy and revelation of His nature out of it as perseverance completes its work. This produces a people who are confident in the goodness of God, they know who they are and that no circumstances will cause them to reinterpret the clear declarations in His Word.

Doubt Arms the Enemy

We had been leading the Body of believers known as Church of the Undignified for seven years and the weekly attendance continued to linger around an average of 35 people. I believe strongly that a church's Sunday morning statistics are not a proclamation of that church's success. Yet it can be very discouraging when you look out and begin to wonder if your presence and effort are doing anything at all. Those very questions emerge in moments of weakness (and honesty) when we allow a spirit of doubt to surface and suffocate the clear promises and call of God over our lives. The enemy will always attempt to lead us to question what God has said. Once I begin to dwell on those doubts I give them power. The once unthreatening enemy has now been armed.

Trying times are the seasons that I'm learning not to just endure but to enjoy, knowing that they are leading me into the throne room, into the nature of Jesus, and into a place where I lack nothing. These are not season that I need to hurry through, but storms I need to learn to rest in, allowing perseverance to finish its work. Jesus was able to sleep in a boat in the middle of a storm without wondering if God was mad. He knew the nature of God and what He wanted to do.

Ones to Imitate

I am fed by the testimonies of church history that tell of small groups of people that believed for something big and didn't abandon the mission as excruciating fires descended. After three years of Jesus' ministry, hundreds of thousands of people getting set free, healed, delivered and hearing the very wisdom of God, only 120 people remained after His resurrection. That's not a great success story if the Man is to be measured by His numbers. The remainder pressed in, giving themselves to prayer and the promises—wait until you've been given the promise of the Holy Spirit and you've been clothed with power from on high—and perseverance reached a breaking point and all heaven broke loose.

During the Welsh Revival, a young man named Evan Roberts preached before an unmoved gathering of 17 people. Pleading for them to give themselves to Jesus, going in and out of prayer, he poured his heart out. Eventually, all 17 people gave themselves to the risen Jesus and Roberts then commented, "We are on the eve of the greatest revival in human history." Faith that comes from God can stand with a sliver of hope and feel the momentum of the Spirit, feast on His promises unswervingly, and know that tremendous breakthrough is coming for "His Word never returns void" and "we will reap a harvest if we do not give up." Feel the certainty of those verses (Is. 55:11; Gal. 6:9). During every fog and storm there will be a point where we hear those verses and we will choose to give them a different meaning, put an asterisk by them, *or* we will strengthen ourselves in its living power, knowing it is truth. Our enduring faith will give life and power to those promises and water the seed of that word.

Promises and Problems

Wherever there is great promise, there will also be great conflict. Since the good of what God has called me to is beyond my ability to comprehend and will, it is also guaranteed to bring me into great testing. For He is not desiring to give great things to immature people who are not yet prepared for the land and influence He has in store for them. He is not in a hurry with me. He would rather I learn the lessons of perseverance sooner than later, but it seems that He will not launch me into a position that I am not poised to carry, having not yet proved faithful in my ability to handle what He has already given me.

Perhaps more than circumstantial conflict, I have witnessed that it is also required that my mind and logic be offended (See Chapter 3). The Lord needs to know if I will follow Him regardless if something makes sense to me. We enter the realm of faith when we step out solely on what He has said to us, trying not to be terrified, but leaning on His Word. We walk by faith—what He has said—and not by sight—the way things appear to our natural senses. When faith is tethered to natural circumstances then endurance will be without the fuel of His perspective. We are motivated and energized by what God is saying as we refuse to allow difficulty to dictate our course of action.

His kingdom requires that we be certain. Be sure of what you're hoping for and certain of what you cannot see (Heb. 11:1). This is faith. Walking by faith is not so much embracing uncertainty as it is becoming friends with the unseen and growing confident in His voice and our ability to hear it. It was such a comfort to me when I understood that faith alone pleases God. It is possible for me to be dead wrong in a decision I've made and still please God if I made the decision from a place of faith as I moved out on what I thought He was telling me. And on the contrary, the pleasure of God does not necessarily rest on someone who is always making the right moves but has neglected to apply faith, apply heaven's direction, or has only moved by reason. Doing the right things does not necessarily please God. "Without faith it is impossible to please Him" (Heb. 11:6). Whatever does not come from faith is sin—missing the mark (Rom. 14:23). Brutal. If we are missing the mark and sinning when not moving from faith, I think we can deduce that we are intended to live every aspect of our lives from a place of certainty and expectation.

God wants me to be confident that I am hearing from Him. He longs for me to move on what I've heard Him say and allow myself to risk, be certain of what I hope for and can't see, giving glory to God. Walking into the deep things of God requires that I become more and more comfortable with putting my weight on what cannot be seen or proved. Doing such things demonstrates our trust in God, His word and that His reality and Word are more important than the way things seem around us.

The Praise of Faith

Romans 4:20 became a critical verse for my life as I felt again and again that I needed to blindly believe God and take Him at

His word. His word over our church was that we would see Isaiah 61 fulfilled in our ministry—broken people would be restored, healed, set free and equipped to bring the kingdom of God to entire cities. When you only see the failures and people not getting free and people leaving your ministry, it is very natural (in the flesh) to begin to question the call, the mission, the word He's spoken, and your own adequacy. But it's in these moments and season, when it appears that all is going the opposite way of the promise, that I am learning to smile, give thanks to God, get strengthened in my expectation of His manifestation in power, knowing He has to show up in order for anything positive to happen. I wouldn't call the attitude desperation. I would call it absolute dependence that is rooted in a faith that is noticed by joyful expectation of His movements.

Just as Abraham did, I needed to not waver in unbelief regarding whether or not what God had said would actually come to pass in my life and through my obedience to Him. I must continuously "strengthen myself in faith giving glory to God" (Romans 4:20) and be fully convinced that what He had promised He is able to perform (v. 21). To be trusted with great promises I learned that I must develop a habit of faith and praise, where, especially in conflicting circumstances, I am habitually drawn to praise for what He is currently blessing and carrying out in my life and gain strength from what He has said. When the circumstances run contrary to the word He's given me, the temptation is to begin to question whether I heard Him right. The moment I doubt the word, I empower the enemy and I step onto an icy slope called fear and unbelief while religion and powerlessness wait at the bottom.

Being far from perfect, Abraham often fell into fear and used lies and deceit to try to protect himself. The father of our faith still had trust issues in many other areas yet he, amazingly, continued to believe God for becoming the father of many nations. He endured for 25 years carrying the promise with expectation. In periods of conflict and adversity he would routinely return to the places where God had encountered him, where he had received promises, and he would call out to God and strengthen himself in what God Himself had spoken to him.

Disappointing Timelines

Telling God how long I'll give Him or what He must do in order for me to keep going usually came from a root of unbelief. I can give many good reasons for my actions and decision but I didn't have to look long in Scripture before I understood that He's not really confined by logic or our inferior, natural reality.

Problems arise when we adjust our expectations in the wake of disappointments. Anyone who has journeyed with God for more than a few years has been disappointed in some area. Perhaps we believed and cried out for something big and yet the answer never came. The healing never happened. What we were certain of did not turn out how we were sure it would. It is in these moments where we often reason ourselves into a lower gospel. We reduce our expectations with a fear that we call wisdom and we stop being ridiculous in our hope. My pursuit of the miracle life of Jesus has taught me that I cannot create a new theology based on my disappointments or what I don't understand. I cannot redefine the nature and will of God by what didn't happen. His nature and will are defined clearly in the person of Jesus. Everything I believe to be true of God must be able to be seen in the life of Jesus.

Being Certain of Fruit

Early in my ministry in Seattle I was comforted with the possibility that I may just be a sower. "One sows and another reaps" (John 4:37). I thought that my purpose might be to just pour myself onto the hardened ground and try to release life and love. For many who struggled with sexual or chemical addictions, when Light and clarity came they realized that they should move out of the Capitol Hill neighborhood. Too many temptations and negative reminders. But my life's purpose is not to be one who endures, but one who reaps a harvest. God is honored when we endure but He is *glorified* when we're fruitful (Jn. 15:8).

My endurance and faith will pursue a life that has the same healing affect around me as Jesus' did. I am destined to become "a mature man, to the measure of the stature which belongs to the fullness of Christ" (Ephesians 4:13). His nature is my destiny, my Promised Land. My experiences do not change the nature and will of God. His nature and goodness are fixed. When things don't line up with His goodness, then I have become okay with living in mystery, not driven to find answers. When tragedies fall and questions ripple out to blur His goodness, I am certain of this: I need more of Him and more of His power on my life, more of His

Spirit, more of His kingdom come.

The Israelites journeyed out of slavery, through the desert and into a real Promised Land. The land was a real place. And what we are enduring toward is something that will be experienced in our life and ministry. It seems that we often get rewarded according to what we have believed for. If I believe that my obedience is only storing up for me something in heaven, but no fruitfulness on earth, then I am not likely to experience much fruit on earth. It's daring to believe. This life is not just about enduring. God is a God of reward and the Fulfiller of promises. Remember, it brings Him glory when we bear fruit and it is in fruitfulness that we show ourselves to be His disciples (John 15:8).

Moses raised this topic with God. Are we really just going to die in the desert? All the nations will laugh at us and ridicule our God. God does not receive the glory He is supposed to when we do not reach our destiny, our Promised Land, the fulfillment of what He has spoken over our lives. And we do a disservice to God when we don't actually believe that He will do what He has said. He has said we have power and authority, but lowering our beliefs because we don't *feel* powerful must grieve the Spirit.

The Goodness of God

I believe that our motivation for enduring is ultimately grounded in our belief in God's good nature. I must know that He's entirely good, incapable of bringing anything that is destructive. Biblical hope is founded on the goodness of God, for enduring and expecting good will only well up within those who are truly convinced of His goodness. If there is any place in our hearts that believes that God would give sickness or cause a tragedy in "judgment", it will affect our ability to hope for good. If we live believing it's possible for Him to do damage then it will be impossible for us to be completely convinced in our hope, rendering us faith-less. I must have a matching confidence in what I believe I have heard Him say to me and over me. I must live expectantly.

If my 4-year-old son, Sam, asked me for a sandwich for him and his friend, I would love to make it for him. Suppose he went back to his neighbor friend and let him know that he asked me for sandwiches for the two of them.

"Did you ask your dad?"

"Yep."

"What did he say?"

"He said he would make us sandwiches."

And suppose a very un-childlike conversation continued:

"Do you think he'll do it?"

"I don't know. I know he is able to do it, but I'm not sure if he'll actually do it."

This sounds so ridiculous, but it is so similar to the "faith" we have in God. We asked Him for something or some influence (and many of those requests have come from His heart having rubbed off on ours) and I reveal my unbelief in His loving, paternal nature when I don't demonstrate any certainty of something being done. It's not that I can order Him around, I am simply aware that I am a son, the Father loves the son and it is His good pleasure to move on his behalf. Not only that, but as a son I have been entrusted with authority and all that belongs to the Father. So there is power in what I say, what I pray and what I declare.

"Son, I love you. If I said I would make you a sandwich then I will." In fact, "ask whatever you want and it will be done for you" (John 15:7).

Childlike faith and endurance will live knowing this verse is true regardless of the times when things seem to backfire. It would be difficult to endure if I ever thought God was throwing wrenches in my spokes. He is not telling me to do something and then sneaking around the corner and opposing me. This is not the image of a loving Father. He is 100% leading me. He is also 100% behind me. He will work everything out for my good and in no way will He be making things more difficult for me than they need to be. My primary fuel is knowing He's a loving, good Father who is battling for my breakthrough into my Promised Land.

The Illusion of Failure

Failure is an illusion, a lie, used by the enemy to trick us into quitting. Entertaining thoughts of failure and receiving them into our lives will have a cancerous effect on our faith and perseverance. Endurance, on the contrary, knows there is no failure when we are moved by faith and obedience.

Grounded in the Unseen

Another key that motivates us to persevere lies in living by the superior realm of the Spirit. I must have the core of my life anchored in the unseen rather than having my faith reduced to what I can understand or weighed down by my disappointing circumstances. It makes the most logical sense that this *spiritual* life will be governed by principles and fruits that are, by nature, spiritual and unseen with the natural eyes. Due to the reality that our *real* lives are hidden with Christ in God, having been rescued from the domain of darkness and transferred into the kingdom of His beloved Son (Col. 3:3; 1:13), we are primarily spirit and not flesh and blood. As Jesus explained the basics to Nicodemus, "That which is born of the Spirit is Spirit" (John 3:6). Upon being "born again", or "born from above", we are invited to live by a new standard of perception, with new wisdom, with the mind of Christ, from kingdom perspective. This is a lifetime journey to enjoy as we learn to hear His voice, live by the truth of our new kingdom environment and exercise dominion and rule with hearts of service and the power of the Spirit.

I've been able to quote "we walk by faith and not by sight ("outward appearance") (2 Cor. 5:7) for as long as I can remember, but living a life that is 100% grounded in the unseen realm is the most absurd and simultaneously most rewarding invitation in this life. Without the gifts of the Spirit and knowing the realities of the realm that contains our real (spiritual) life, we are of little use to the kingdom of God. All believers have been transferred into His kingdom (Col.

1:13), and yet when I lived primarily aware of my natural world I was functionally worldly and not spiritual. This provided me with a better explanation of why I was having so little impact on the world around me. I was being called to a higher level, to live from the life and kingdom that Jesus had purchased for me. Seeing from His perspective and understanding what He has freely given us (1 Cor. 2:12) provides me with all the incentive I need in any given circumstance or situation.

To be Christian means that we will live not only valuing some *One* but some *things* that we cannot prove. In other words, we are to live by a reality and presence that we cannot see in order that we may experience that which we are hoping for. We are invited to live in hope and faith, which long to experience realities that are presently eluding us.

Hope Defined

> "For in hope we have been saved, but hope that is seen is not hope; for who hopes for what he already sees? But if we hope for what we do not see, with perseverance we wait eagerly for it" (Romans 8:24, 25).

To live in hope means that we are in hot pursuit of something that is not known in the natural. We carry a conviction of a superior truth in our hearts and our persevering faith is what pulls on His kingdom and brings His reality into ours. "With perseverance we wait eagerly" for what we do not yet experience of His promises. Applying this with an example, it means that if Jesus says we have all authority and power then we persevere eagerly toward this reality without lowering the standard Jesus has set for us as He routinely and consistently healed and set free everyone (Acts 10:38). The volume of His truth must be turned louder than the questions in my head.

When we encounter disappointments there is usually a blow that is dealt to our faith and certainty. We usually become less likely to dream big or believe big. We've been let down and where we were once sure of what God wanted to do, we become uncertain of His will. Persevering means we will continue to hope big and not let up. Our disappointments don't lower the standard but serve as fuel to our appetite for more of His nature to be formed in us.

During 2011 I spent many occasions by the deathbeds of others, releasing life and healing, coming against the injustice of sickness and disease as the enemy was doing what he does—stealing, killing and destroying. All of those battles I "lost". The people died. Had Jesus been there they would not have died. Rather than feeling guilt and shame, knowing the lack was on my end and not God's, I was driven to fast and press in for more of God and His nature to be realized in me. I hunger for the impact of Jesus' life to have the same effect around me as it did around Him. In the emotion of coming up short we have the choice of concluding that God is not in this and we can shift directions or scale our dreams back so they are more reasonable, or we learn the basic biblical principles of faith, hope and perseverance.

If I am hoping for what I do not yet see (i.e. have any "hope" at all), I am instructed in the verse above, "with perseverance we wait eagerly for it." This "waiting" means that we are diligently looking for the fulfillment. To live with hope implies that we will be perseveringly longing for a fulfillment.

Endurance Understands Process

> Tribulation brings about perseverance; and perseverance, proven character; and proven character, hope; and hope does not disappoint (make ashamed), because the love of God has been poured out within our hearts through the Holy Spirit whom He has given us (Romans 5:3-5).

In Romans 5 we learn a different aspect and nature of hope. According to this passage hope is not just something that you choose to have but it is a fruit and result of faith-based endurance, which is committed to a process.

If we have been embarrassed or disappointed by what we have hoped for then we do not understand the nature of God or the principle of perseverance. Romans 5:5 reveals the fact that hope does not "make ashamed" or "disappoint". And Paul backs this statement with the reason that God's love has already been poured out into our hearts by His very Presence, the Holy Spirit. With God's very Presence, His nature, the Comforter, who reveals truth and the thoughts of God living inside us, how would it be possible to fall into shame or disappointment? Living aware of His Presence within will topple any tendencies toward discouragement or lowering our expectation in the shadow of failure or looming disappointments.

Endurance lives under the revelation that we are all on a journey into perfection. We are leaning in toward the coming of His kingdom in fullness and it is our expectation of that completeness that makes us dissatisfied with lack and keeps us pressing in toward our goal and assignment—to bring heaven to earth.

Still the Shaken

While I was once fueling our car at a gas station, a man came out of the station's store shaking his head violently back and forth. He walked toward me continuing to uncontrollably whip his head side to side. I asked him how he was doing and he asked me for money. I took hold of his hand in the form of a handshake and his head movements slowed. We hugged and then he asked me for a kiss as he continued to speak rapidly and franticly. I smiled, declined and then pulled him close and began to whisper peace and the love Jesus into his ear. He exhaled several times and grew silent and still as the presence of the Holy Spirit settled on his fractured soul.

I had a powerful encounter with that man, but he was still spiritually harassed when he walked away from me. That moment of peace was brief for him and I knew believers were capable of releasing a more complete healing to such tormented individuals. My hope is to be able to minister in the same fashion as Jesus. His life is what I'm yearning for. My perseverance is stretching toward *His* normal. There is a measure of disappointment I experience when people do not get healed when I pray over them because His will is healing. The lack is on my end. I long for His nature to be fully formed in me. My shortcomings continue to feed my hunger for more of God.

Supernatural Hope

Biblical hope is something that comes upon a person by the power of the Holy Spirit. Paul prays in Romans 15:13 saying, "May the God of hope fill you with all joy and peace in believing, so that you will abound in hope by the power of the Holy Spirit." I believe that this verse pieces it all together for us. We serve the God of hope (Who confidently expects good) and it is His intention that, as we press in for what we do not see, we are filled with *all* joy and peace in our believing. This will result in abounding in the gift of hope by the power of the Holy Spirit.

Endurance in our faith (carrying on being certain of what we cannot see) releases joy and peace upon us. Persevering expectation releases His kingdom on us because the kingdom of God consists of peace and joy (Rom. 14:17) and faith is what pleases God. As we persevere in what we are hoping for, it is God's desire to load us up with peace and joy as we press in. Endurance does not have to be horrible. It is not only possible but divinely preferred that we enjoy peace and laughter in seasons that demand so much spiritual strength and resolve. The end result is that we are overflowing with hope. It is this kind of hope within us that will see destinies fulfilled, cities changed and a momentum of righteousness that is without end.

The underlying principle is that there is no fulfillment without perseverance. Disappointments and dead ends cannot sway faith, redefine dreams or lower hopes. It is impossible for hope to disappoint us (Romans 5:5). If we ever feel God has let us down then our perspective has to change. There's no other alternative if we desire to remain in faith. Press in on sheer faith and feel His pleasure. Enduring faith moves in expectation that is often void of emotion because it is based solely on the living and piercing words of God. His Word must be more real than the ground we walk on and the bread we chew.

"So That..."

Describing Abraham, it is said that against all hope he believed, in hope, "so that he might become the father of many nations" (Romans 4:18). Hope and perseverance in believing, set against "the odds" (the natural elements that contradict), are the keys that open the doors to destiny and promises fulfilled. Fulfilled promises and destinies lie through the threshold labeled illogical hope. When all the natural elements shouted against the Word hanging over Abraham, he believed anyway. This believing, which God called righteousness, is what enabled him to experience the promise over his life.

Living toward this richness of life is not supposed to be a chore but a thrill. "Rejoicing in hope" is to describe our lives (Romans 12:12).

The Will and the Way

We often carry the idea that if it's God's will then it will occur without a fight and without effort because He has "destined" it to be. Our involvement is "rest and just let Him do it." But we're informed in Hebrews 10 that we need a ton of patience and endurance so that *we* may accomplish the will of God and receive what He's promised.

> "Do not, therefore, fling away your fearless confidence, for it carries a great and glorious compensation of reward. For you have need of steadfast patience and endurance, so that you may perform and fully accomplish the will of God, and thus receive and carry away [and enjoy to the full] what is promised" (Heb. 10:35-36 AMP).

We receive promises through endurance and faith, not because God has sovereignly destined us to obtain a promise. There is a violence to faith. It throws off everything that hinders, it is disgusted by unbelief and presses on unswervingly toward the promise and the eternal realm where the promise was birthed and received.

Any faith that will change the course of history will defy logic. Defying logic looks like foolishness to Western society. We open ourselves to ridicule anytime we value something unseen above the facts that exists in the natural realm. Being seen as delusional or naïve is an understandable judgment. Along with the crazy looks we get there will be an option to alter our course to please others and seem less ridiculous, or we can choose to ignore the projected dishonor.

> "Let us run with endurance the race that is set before us, fixing our eyes on Jesus, the author and perfecter of faith, who for the joy set before Him endured the cross, despising the shame, and has sat down at the right hand of the throne of God" (Hebrews 12:1-2).

Wherever endurance is required there will be a looming shame that is vying for your life and faith. It is voice from hell that breathes the words of failure, abdication, abandonment and giving up.

"Take an easier route."

"This is obviously not God's will."

"What are you doing, Noah, Moses, Gideon, Abraham, Elijah?!" They were all ridiculed for hope, but they, like Jesus, disregarded the shame and confusion that came from the outside or even from within.

Jesus was able to endure the cross and all the sin of humanity on His shoulders because He had His mind fixed on the joy that was set before Him. He knew what His obedience would be purchasing for us—freedom, salvation, healing, power, authority and a current seat in heaven. Motivation for endurance comes when there's clarity on purpose. And as Jesus was focused on the joy set before Him He was simultaneously choosing to "despise the shame." It could be translated that Jesus held the shame in contempt or didn't think about it at all.[13]

---

13 http://www.blueletterbible.org/lang/lexicon/lexicon.cfm?Strongs=G2706&t=NASB

He thought little or nothing of the shame. What is shameful to those living by the reasoning of man is understandable to the spiritual man who has his mind fixed on "things above" (Col. 3:1-2). Much of our spiritual success in endurance has to do with keeping our mind and thoughts on what God has promised and "set before us." We cannot afford to give our thought life over to the faithless, logical input and insults of man. Giving ear to these words poisons the promise and slimes our expectation with uncertainty.

Jesus thought little or nothing about the shame associated with the cross. He knew He would be mocked for saving others yet not saving Himself. But He didn't allow confusion about the necessity of the cross to cloud his faith, joy and expectancy.

Focus

Church History is decorated with men and women of faith who pushed through shame and modeled a quality of life that affected multitudes. One of the greatest healing revivalists in history was John G. Lake. Yet in his life he watched as eight of his siblings were taken by sickness and disease. His own wife was taken by sickness. Refusing to change the message and reduce the Word to his experience, he endured and went on to found the Healing Rooms, which transformed the city of Spokane, Washington into the "healthiest city in America."[14] When so many of his loved ones had died of illness he chose to press in for the healing gift and

---

14 Roberts Liardon, "Why They Succeeded and Why Some Failed," *God's Generals*, (New Kensington, PA: Whitaker House, 1996), p. 189.

engage with those who were seeing breakthrough. While misery often loves the company of those who are also miserable, revivalists will seek out those who are experiencing abundant life.

My need to press in toward the promise and not meditate on the natural "evidences" that shouts the contrary may be the most prominent theme of my life. There is a race/fight/struggle that is set before each of us, which we are destined for. Whether or not to engage cannot be a choice that I entertain. Doing nothing with the resources (and Spirit) that God gives us is not an option. The parable of the talents shows God's thoughts in the matter. Those who live by the truth of a greater reality enjoy the rich promises of God that bring heaven's reality to earth. They feed on words that come from the mouth of God and are deaf to the ridicule that our absurd faith naturally brings forth. Reckless, persevering faith will always expose unbelief, be mocked, and make others uncomfortable and nervous.

The Body

In order to persevere in a life of faith that will establish the kingdom of God, it is a necessity to be intimately involved in a Body of believers. While we walk the edge of what is faith and what is outright stupid, it is beyond helpful to have a community of believers around us who also demonstrate and value the heavenly realm and God's voice above the natural realm. We are all too human and if we attempt this spiritual life alone, we are inviting disaster to dinner.

Making the Leap

Making the leap into the unknown, into the supernatural, into faith and into His kingdom is perilous. But I'm convinced that more is at stake when we avoid such a risk. Many misunderstanding, accusations and eye-rolls follow those brass enough to believe that Jesus was a model for what our lives are to look like. Making the transition is not an option. The kingdom of God comes in power or it doesn't come at all (1 Cor. 4:20). Spending my life of ministry *not* bringing the kingdom would be splendidly stupid. So let's step out.

Surprised by Joy

I learned during my transition, as Church of the Undignified became a community who celebrated the gifts and the presence of God, that joy was a frequent byproduct of God's nearness. When He began to touch people, they got happy. Joaquin Evans was the first person to teach me "seriousness is not a fruit of the Spirit." Rejoicing carries joy. If God is in a room and people are rejoicing before Him, it makes good sense that there would be a heavy manifestation of joy. If people are *full* of joy, this means that joy is coming *out*. What do we do when joy comes out? We laugh.

"In Your presence is fullness of joy" (Ps. 16:11). Complete joy describes the presence of God. If God comes to our Sunday meetings then it should be no surprise if people are happy, laughing and enjoying themselves as He draws nearer and nearer. When we gather together we know that, "to each one is given the manifestation of the Spirit for the common good" (1 Cor. 12:7). This means that if someone is manifesting joy as God joins our meeting then that joy is present for the common good. When joy and laughter are falling on someone, that joy has just become available for everyone present to partake of. Someone may get a breakthrough into freedom, and now freedom has just been released in the room. Every manifestation of the Spirit comes to pass for the common good. Yet if we call a manifestation into question then we are only limiting our ability to benefit from that manifestation of the Spirit and we may, tragically and inadvertently, put ourselves out of the reach of the Spirit's blessing. One of the best ways to be blessed by God's activity is to celebrate with those who are encountering Him and receive, in faith, the benefit of their encounter.

When Abbi and I went to our first "charismatic" conference she made note of one particular manifestation that she didn't care to experience. It seemed that when some people were "touched" by God they would convulse in their stomachs. Their heads would dart forward as if they were just poked in the abdomen with a tack. Abbi referred to this reaction as the "chicken dance". "God", she said, "I want all of You, I just don't want to do the chicken dance." On the last day of the conference, she was at the front and the joy of God came over her. The Spirit started to move on her and, yes, she was convulsing like a chicken. As the glory and presence of God became so unbearably heavy on her she gave in and went to the ground. She was on the floor for 45 minutes, laughing tears. Her encounter with Father God that night changed her forever. Internal issues that she had struggled with for years had been healed in a moment in the loving presence of Him who comes in ways outside our choosing.

Choices, Choices

Clearly, the Spirit can stir things up. The presence of God does not come just so we can be happy. He comes to heal and equip us. He comes to form God's nature in us and clothe us with power from on high. He comes to make us capable of re-presenting Christ and establishing His kingdom on the earth.

I can be very orderly in some of my approaches to life. But the Spirit cannot be operative under restrictions. "Where the Spirit of the Lord is, there is liberty" (2 Cor. 3:17). Because God's presence demands freedom I knew that our meetings had to truly be committed to His lead. The Spirit can indeed be restricted by humanity, and our ability to hear and cooperate with His movements. I had to be more than *okay* with Him showing up, releasing freedom and joy in the room. It may seem disorderly, chaotic or uncomfortably loud. But what is my desire in our Sunday meetings anyway? That people are comfortable? *No*, I am primarily concerned that people encounter God when we gather together.

So, on occasions there have been people laughing uncontrollably, and we'll just pause and allow the Spirit to do what He's doing. We may explain to the group that joy is being released and invite everyone to receive it.

There were many choices to make as I sought the presence of God. I also felt I had a responsibility to lead and grow Church of the Undignified. And as new people come into the theater it is possible that they will find people acting as though they are drunk. We are also a Body who likes to have fun, so when people enter they may witness others actually having fun in church. But my desire that visitors feel welcomed and comfortable in church had to take a far back seat to the Holy Spirit. I have learned to trust that if people are hungry then they will recognize the presence of the One they crave. I do not want to control the Spirit, manipulate people into staying at our church by pretending to be "normal", or sand the edges off of our vicious gospel. Many people left our church when we kept talking about the kingdom of God and our responsibility to usher it in with the power of God. The healing ministry of Jesus had captivated me and, for a season, there was nothing else I could preach. Yet I had decided that pursuing *this gospel* was the very purpose of our church.

I love coming to church and not knowing what's going to happen! I'm not in charge. I may have a plan or an "order of service" in hand, but the best Sundays are when that gets thrown out the window because the glory of God fills the room. Jesus gave us the job of bringing the kingdom while He took on the responsibility of building the church (Luke. 10:9; Mt. 16:18). My primary concern is the kingdom of God and the movements of the Spirit, not making sure people are comfortable in church. When I reversed those directives I only revealed my lack of confidence in the Spirit. I not only want Him there, I want Him to come in power, shake the room, equip us and fill us. The Sunday I don't expect that to happen will be dreadfully boring.

I'll Have What They're Having

Just before Jesus ascended, the disciples were given the instructions to stay in the city and wait for what the Father had promised. The message of the kingdom and of salvation was burning in their hands and yet they were not to go anywhere or preach a word until they got "the promise". "You will receive power when the Holy Spirit has come upon you; and you shall be My witnesses both in Jerusalem, and in all Judea and Samaria, and even to the remotest parts of the earth" (Acts. 1:8). Before they went to the nations with the greatest news known to mankind they had to be immersed in the Holy Spirit (Acts 1:5). Power had to be on them because power is the defining mark of the message of the kingdom of God (1 Cor. 4:20).

So they wait. They wait in "one accord" and "one mind". They waited with what was likely the most dangerous prayer meeting in history. "These all with one mind were continually devoting themselves to prayer" (Acts 1:14). The word translated, "one mind", is the word ὁμοθυμαδόν. This comes from the two words, ὁμοῦ (which means "together") and θυμός (which means "passion, angry, heat, fierceness")[15]. This gathering and waiting that ushered in the fire of God's empowering Spirit was marked by a unity and a fiery passion that could actually be confused with anger. I imagine them shouting and pounding the ground, crying out for the Spirit. They had to get out of the city with this message but they were

---

[15] http://www.blueletterbible.org/lang/lexicon/lexicon.cfm?Strongs=G3661&t=NASB

instructed not to. A passion for His kingdom boiled within them and they craved the Spirit and His accompanying power.

It was still as death but then there was the sound of a strong wind that filled the room. Something like fire fell on each of them, the Holy Spirit filled them, and they began to speak of the powerful acts of God in other languages. To those perceiving them with natural eyes, they looked drunk.

Goodbye Dignity

I have become convinced that in order to walk as Jesus did, with miracles and wonders, then we have to deal with our fear of looking stupid. I cannot be concerned with looking foolish, being misunderstood, or being palatable. I want to be dangerous to darkness and bring His kingdom to the earth. And if I look drunk while I'm doing it, so be it. I want the Spirit all over me and I *have* to see His kingdom come in power.

In the first years of my search for more of God and the miracle life of Jesus, I found myself being pounded by a line from *When Heaven Invades Earth*. The author describes His own search for more explaining, "At the forefront was the realization that God wanted to make an exchange—His increased presence for my dignity."[16] As pastor of Church of the *Undignified*, dignity was something that I knew had to be on the altar. The Holy Spirit was near in that

16 Bill Johnson, *When Heaven Invades Earth*, (Shippensurg, PA: Destiny Image Publishers, 2003), p. 62.

moment and I knew that I was on the right track. Not only did I want to move in power but I also knew that God *wanted* me to walk in a supernatural fashion. And He had made every provision necessary for me to live miraculously. I called out to Him, and he replied with a fire of power. It is consuming me and creating a wildfire in my city and spreading to nations. I am overcome with thoughts and dreams of His kingdom coming in power and I can feel His smile over me as I live toward the standard that Jesus set.

"…and He healed them all" (Matthew 12:15).

THE LAST WORD

The good news, as it is seen, felt and heard with power and miracles, will cause the darkest places on earth to become revival-training centers. "If the miracles had been performed in Tyre and Sidon which occurred in you, they would have repented long ago" (Luke 10:13). Jesus explains that the miracle lifestyle will transform our most oppressed cities. Sodom, Tyre and Sidon would've soon repented if they were witnessing great miracles. The context of this passage seems to be indicating that the people of rebellious cities will not be blamed if there has been no *demonstration* of the Good News. "Sorry, they didn't know any better. They never saw the power of God. If they did, they would've have changed." Hear this again: Jesus said that these cities would've changed if they saw miracles. From the outset miracles have been intended to be used by people moving in the power of God to usher in His kingdom, and allow His love to be experienced. In the wake of miracles we will likely find cities and nations transformed through proofs of God's reality and *objectively good* nature.

Let the fun begin.